PINK
FLOYD
THE
EARLY
YEARS

OMNIBUS PRESS

London • New York • Paris • Sydney • Copenhagen • Berlin • Madrid • Tokyo

BARRY MILES

PINK
FLOYD
THE
EARLY
YEARS

ISBN 13: 978.1.84609.444.6
ISBN 1.84609.444.5
Order No: OP51480

Exclusive Distributors
Music Sales Limited,
14/15 Berners Street,
London W1T 3LJ, UK

Music Sales Corporation,
257 Park Avenue South,
New York, NY 10010, USA

Macmillan Distribution Services,
53 Park West Drive,
Derrimut, Vic 3030,
Australia

To the Music Trade only:
Music Sales Limited,
14/15 Berners Street,
London W1T 3LJ, UK

Every effort has been made to trace the copyright holders of the photographs in this book but one or two were unreachable. We would be grateful if the photographers concerned would contact us.

Book designed by:
Matt Brown, Designbranch

Cover designed by:
Michael Brown Design

Printed in the United States of America

A catalog record for this book is available from the British Library.

Visit Omnibus Press on the web
at www.omnibuspress.com

08 CHAPTER ONE
CAMBRIDGE
22 CHAPTER TWO
SYD & DAVID
34 CHAPTER THREE
THE MOVE TO TOWN
48 CHAPTER FOUR
UNDERGROUND LONDON
60 CHAPTER FIVE
LONDON FREE SCHOOL
& INTERNATIONAL TIMES
74 CHAPTER SIX
UFO CLUB
86 CHAPTER SEVEN
FROM ARNOLD TO EMILY
100 CHAPTER EIGHT
ON THE ROAD
112 CHAPTER NINE
DAVID JOINS
122 CHAPTER TEN
MEET THE NEW BOSS
136 CHAPTER ELEVEN
ATOM HEART MOTHER TO MEDDLE
146 CHAPTER TWELVE
DARK SIDE OF THE MOON

CHAPTER ONE
CAMBRIDGE

CHAPTER ONE
CAMBRIDGE

Despite pressure from property developers, Grantchester Meadows remains a quintessentially English patch of countryside, with muddy paths showing the passage of ducks and foxes, dogs and people, lone fishermen on the banks of the winding River Cam, distant bells from the massed church spires beyond the trees, and everywhere the sound of birdsong. The City of Cambridge is relatively small, around 100,000 people, and is one of the most beautiful cities in Britain, if not the world. It has a very powerful physical presence and visitors cannot avoid feeling a tremendous sense of continuity with the past.

All art forms contain an element of the environment that created them, including rock and roll: Elvis Presley was a southern boy, Fats Domino and Dr John have the deep rolling sound of New Orleans, The Beatles were clearly from Liverpool just as the Rolling Stones were the sound of the London suburbs – and Pink Floyd were from Cambridge. Nick Mason and Rick Wright, of course, came from London but the three successive leaders and principal songwriters of the band: Syd Barrett, Roger Waters and David Gilmour were all Cantabrigians.

Elements of their childhood in that city impose themselves on Pink Floyd music in all three of its linked incarnations. No matter how indifferent you may be to ancient buildings it is impossible to spend time in Cambridge without the environment of solid stone walls, the classical volumes and proportions of the buildings, the medieval arrangement of streets and alleys, and the rich patina of age slowing your step, making you aware of the past and reducing the urgency of the present. In the town centre it is still common to see masters and students in gowns and even the occasional mortarboard, the Cam is still thronged with students in punts, and bicycles far outnumber cars in the narrow winding streets of the centre. The country is never far away and the Backs provide an arboreal setting for endless picture postcard views. Ancient bells still ring out from medieval towers and the atmosphere is liturgical: one of learning, of respect for learning; of being part of an historical process.

It is this physical environment, rather than the aural environment (car radios, TV ads) which most American groups had, that is echoed in the architectural structures suggested by Pink Floyd's music. Even Syd Barrett showed preference for long improvisational passages defined more by surfaces and textures than by virtuoso guitar pyrotechnics. Roger Waters was the most obviously architectural in the construction of his music but Rick Wright and Nick Mason shared his approach – all three were architectural students, of course – down to planning songs with diagrams and graphs rather than words scribbled in pencil on the back of an envelope. Even with master rock guitarist Gilmour at the helm, the music suggests the enormous volumes of architecture and is more likely to proceed at the stately pace of a hymn than a Chuck Berry duckwalk.

As with many groups, the line-up of Pink Floyd was the result of the successive shuffling of players in a series of bands who joined, left and exchanged members in a formal dance that left a lucky few holding a full dance card. On the floor were a circle of friends and acquaintances who knew each other at school in Cambridge and, in many cases, whose parents also knew each other. Various Cambridge, then London-based, groups maneuvered until the band took its final shape. Some of these people played a brief role then moved on, others took on new roles, such as art direction or spouse, while one, David Gilmour, tried a different route before being asked to dance.

ROGER WATERS

George Roger Waters was born on September 9, 1943, the youngest of three boys, in the village of Great Bookham, Surrey, near Dorking, about 20 miles south of London. His father Eric Fletcher Waters, a religious education and physical education teacher, was in Italy serving in the armed forces as a Second Lieutenant with the City of London Regiment of the 8th Battalion Royal Fusiliers under General Leese. His unit was among those that managed a successful landing on January 22 on the beaches at Anzio, 60 miles north of Cassino. This landing behind enemy lines was designed to

Above: Roger (back row, far left) as part of 'The County' High School rugby team, 1960.

'A big bonfire, and being held up to the window, and people with flags... and dancing, and flickering light.'

Roger Waters

draw German forces away from the Cassino front so that British and American troops could break through and head north to Rome. The beachhead was consolidated but unfortunately did not break out to engage enemy forces. Parts of the German 14th army were rushed to Anzio as anticipated but they were able to contain the beachhead and pinned down British and American forces in a stalemate. Then, on February 18, 1944, as the allies bombed Monte Cassino prior to the second battle for the ancient monastery, Eric Waters was shot and killed. Roger was five months old.

As if life was not hard enough for the Waters family, on June 13, 1944, the Germans began launching doodlebugs – V1 flying bombs – against London, many of which overflew Surrey. Several thousand were shot down by artillery or by fighter planes before they reached London, making their flight paths a treacherous place to live. Mary Waters packed her belongings and took her sons, John, the eldest, Duncan and Roger, to Cambridge to start a new life. Roger was two years old. His earliest memory is of VJ night, August 15, 1945: "A big bonfire, and being held up to the window, and people with flags... and dancing, and flickering light." It was only when his schoolmates began to be picked up from nursery school by their fathers in 1946 when the troops were demobbed that he began asking where *his* father was. When it sank in that he was dead, Roger became very agitated. His absent father eventually came to dominate his life; becoming the theme for some of his best, and his most obsessional work.

Roger was born into an old-style, resolutely left-wing family. His paternal grandparents lived at Copley, near Barnard Castle in County Durham where his grandmother was the housekeeper for the local country doctor. His grandfather was a coal miner in the drift mines and then became the Labour Party agent for Bradford before dying in the trenches of the Great War. Roger's father, Eric Fletcher Waters, grew up as a communist Christian, as Waters told the *Daily Telegraph*: "You could not fail to be a communist then. The children of Bradford did not have shoes or clogs but rags about their feet." The sacrifice made by both his grandfather and his father was burned into his psychic makeup and was to profoundly affect his life: "I'm filled with the sense that I am heir to their passion and my forebears' commitment to right and wrong, to truth and justice. I hope I have inherited what I admire about them as men, that they had the courage of their convictions, which caused them to give their lives for liberty and freedom."

Mary Waters hailed from Scotland, a Communist Party member until the Russian invasion of Hungary in 1956 which turned many people away from the party. She became a strong supporter of the post-war Labour government and was very involved in local politics. Somehow she managed the daunting tasks of bringing up three boys, holding down her job as a teacher at Morley Memorial Junior School, and being actively engaged in a number of left-wing and humanitarian causes. Roger's childhood was filled with meetings at the Quaker Meeting House and the Anglo-Chinese Friendship Association, demos and hours of earnest talk. Roger told Jim Ladd: "I think that she gave me, in lots of ways, a reasonable view of the world and what it was like – or as reasonable as she could. Nevertheless, I think that parents tend to indoctrinate their children with their own beliefs far too strongly. My mother was extremely left wing and I grew up really believing that left wing politics was where it was at. But of course, all the children of right wing parents all held the opposite view. And it's very difficult for parents to say to their children, 'Well now, this is what I believe, but I might well be wrong.' Because they don't feel they're wrong. They've sorted it out and they feel they're right, but I think you can waste an awful lot of your life if you just adopt your parents' view of the world – or if you reject it completely as well. If you use their view either positively or negatively to the exclusion of thinking it out for yourself, you can waste 10 or 15 years like that."

CAMBRIDGE
PINK FLOYD SITES

Clockwise from top left: Syd Barrett's first childhood home at 60 Glisson Road; Homerton Teachers Training College, Hills Road, where pre-teen Roger, Syd and David attended art classes; 'The County' High School, Hills Road, where Roger and Syd studied; Syd's family home, 138 Hills Road where Syd practised with David Gilmour; Grantchester Meadows – the inspiration for many Floyd songs; Morley Memorial Junior School where Roger's mother taught both Roger and Syd; 42 Rock Road where Roger grew up.

'I spent many, many happy hours fishing... in that bit of the river Cam. I have powerful memories of the warmth of summer mud oozing up between my toes. That time turned out to be creatively important for me – my work is coloured to a certain extent by the sound of natural history.'

Roger Waters

His mother was clearly a very strong woman; she had to be in her situation, but Roger had an ambivalent relationship with her. There was always the problem of the missing father, an absence she could not hide from her children. Roger: "For one reason or another, I had some powerful feelings of abandonment when I was a very young child." Roger's song, 'Mother' on *The Wall* addressed some of these problems. He told Jim Ladd: "It's about how parents start inducing, almost inject, their own fears and worries into their children from a very early age. Particularly in my case when they had just been through a world war or something like that – we all go through devastating experiences and we tend to pass them onto our children when they are very young – I suspect." Having lost her husband, Mary Waters was understandably over-possessive of her remaining family, and attempted to exert too much control over their lives. Talking about the song 'Mother,' Roger told DJ Tommy Vance: "If you can level one accusation at mothers it is that they tend to protect their children too much. Too much and for too long. This isn't a portrait of my mother although one or two of the things in there apply to her as well as to, I'm sure, lots of other people's mothers."

The family lived at 42 Rock Road, a pleasant street of small three story houses originally known by their names – Roger's was 'Fleetwood' – off Cherry Hinton Road, just a short distance from some of the most idyllic and beautiful countryside in Britain. Roger would cycle out to Grantchester Meadows and fish for gudgeon and roach with a piece of bread on a bent pin on a bamboo pole and go bird-nesting in the beech woods: "I spent many, many happy hours fishing... in that bit of the river Cam. I have powerful memories of the warmth of summer mud oozing up between my toes. That time turned out to be creatively important for me — my work is coloured to a certain extent by the sound of natural history."

'The Old Vicarage, Grantchester', Rupert Brooks' most famous and memorable

Above left:
The 1964 line-up
of what became
Pink Floyd. L-R:
Syd Barrett,
Bob Klose,
Chris Dennis,
Roger Waters.

Above: Syd
playing with
Those Without,
Cambridge,
January 2, 1965.
L-R: Syd, 'Smudge',
Stephen Pyle,
unknown.

poem, is about his house in Grantchester, a village in easy walking distance of Cambridge, as it was before World War I. Some of its arboreal lyricism rubbed off on Roger, particularly in his song 'Grantchester Meadows.'

Mary Waters also taught at her son's primary school, Morley Memorial Primary on Blinco Grove, which was just around the corner, so he was rarely out of her sight or control. The friendship group that formed the Pink Floyd* began early. When he was eight Roger attended a Saturday morning art class one block away, on the other side of Hills Road at the Homerton Teachers Training College. Among those daubing the gouache and making crocodiles out of clay were both six-year-old Syd Barrett, who was also taught by Roger's mother at Morley Memorial, and David Gilmour. David and Syd were the same age so they became friends, Roger was older, he knew Syd through his mother, and sometimes saw him when he was taken to visit his aunt who lived at 187 Hills Road, two doors from Syd, but being two years older, Roger was naturally too grand to play with the younger boys at school.

Like virtually every other British rock and roller of his generation, Roger spent hours listening through the static to Radio Luxembourg, where raw American rock 'n' roll was beamed at Britain each evening from 6pm accompanied by Horace Bachelor's interminable ads for his Infra-Draw method for winning the football pools.* After frequent time checks, always made on an H. Samuels 'Ever-right watch', it was possible to hear such shows as Alan Freed's *Rock 'n' Roll House Party* the likes of which could not conceivably be broadcast by the staid BBC. Freed nearly always played the original black versions of songs, rather than the pallid white imitations, so his listeners knew about the Chords' 'Sh-Boom (Life Could Be A Dream)' rather than the Crew Cuts; Little Richard sang 'Long Tall Sally' rather than pale, lifeless Pat Boone; and naturally, he played the American releases of songs, not English covers.

Roger: "I remember when I was 10 or 11 listening to Radio Luxembourg on a crystal set with two headphones and the quality was appalling. But listening to early Gene Vincent and early rock and roll hidden under the bed covers still creating magic moments."* Some nights the reception on Radio Luxembourg was bad enough to be unlistenable so the alternative was to tune into the American Armed Forces Network in Frankfurt where rock 'n' roll was interspersed by army news about exercises and new pension directives from the Pentagon. No one would have even considered tuning in to the BBC. The BBC played very little in the way of rock 'n' roll, and certainly not the original black American versions. Most popular hits were covered by one of the BBC's in-house bands like the NDO (the Northern Dance Orchestra) who I once heard grind their way through Little Richard's 'Tutti Frutti' of all things. It was almost unrecognisable.

As he grew older there were also concerts to attend. Roger: "Cambridge was a university town, and there were lots of trad-jazz bands, when I was 11... 12... 13... 14. Mainly it was trad-jazz and I used to go to dances in the Corn Exchange. I'd stand there at the back, and look at the guy playing the trumpet on the stage, and think 'Jesus, that looks good fun. I'd like to be him. I want to be that person.' Maybe that was something that was very likely to happen in Cambridge, and not so likely to happen in Warrington, or Middlesborough, or somewhere up north." He began to buy blues albums by Billie Holiday, Leadbelly and Bessie Smith, but however interested he was in music he made no moves in that direction, something which he also blamed, in part, on Mary Waters. "My mother didn't encourage my creativity," he complained. "She claims to be tone deaf, whatever that means, and has no interest in music and art or anything like that. She's only interested in politics. I didn't really have a happy childhood."

Wilful and opinionated Roger may have seemed to others but he was no match for his mother. Roger's problems with his controlling matriarch no doubt say a lot about his future difficulties with Pink Floyd and with women. In several interviews he revealed that his mother attempted to control his love life, trying to get him to play around rather than get too involved with one person. Roger told KMET's Jim Ladd in 1980: "I think she was kind of old fashioned enough to think that what would be really bad for me would be to find a nice clean girl and get married – and get hooked into some relationship when I was too young. Which in fact, I did. But that's another story. I can remember her specifically actually encouraging me to go out and look for dirty girls... That was a bit more control. It's up to you. What you want to do with women is your affair unless you want to seek somebody's advice. You don't want somebody watching you. I didn't anyway. Especially not your mother."

42 Rock Road was situated just around the corner from 'The County' High School

Above: The embryonic Pink Floyd in the garden of their landlord (and occasional keyboardist)

Mike Leonard's Highgate home, 1965. L–R: Roger, Nick Mason, Syd, Bob Klose, Rick Wright.

*In their early years, approximately
up to when Syd Barrett left the group
in early 1968, Pink Floyd were known
(and generally referred to) as *The* Pink
Floyd. For the chronological purposes
of this book, the prefix will continue
until that time.
*Batchelor's address in Keynsham,
Bristol, was so fixed in the collective
memory from this period that in 1969,
the Bonzo Dog Band titled an album
Keynsham.
*'Be Bop A Lula' was in the charts
in July 1956 so he would have been
almost 13.

on Hills Road. The Cambridgeshire High School For Boys has been the subject of
much vituperation on the part of Roger Waters and can be credited as his main source
of inspiration for *The Wall*; if a deep, seething resentment can be called inspiration:
"Apart from games, which I loved, I loathed every single second of it." In the Fifties,
grammar schools were run very much as they had been before the war: the teachers
had total authority and pupils were expected to do as they were told without question
and to remain silent. However Britain had changed and young people now felt that
they had a right to air their views. When that was resolutely forbidden, their energy
channelled itself in other directions: "It erupted into a very organised clandestine
property violence against the school, with bombs, though nobody ever got hurt."
There was one member of staff, the groundsman, that the pupils decided needed to
be taught a lesson. He was very proud of his apple orchard and there was one tree
in particular, laden with Golden Delicious apples, that was his pride and joy. One
night about 10 of the pupils, including Roger, arrived at the orchard carrying step
ladders and meticulously ate all of the apples, leaving just the cores hanging from
the branches. Roger: "The next morning was just wonderful; we were terribly tired
but filled with a real sense of achievement."

19

The teachers appeared to be simply going through the motions; they made no effort to encourage the children, to praise any of their efforts, or develop any latent talents they might have. Roger told Tommy Vance: "There were some at my school who were just incredibly bad and treated the children so badly, just putting them down, putting them down, you know, all the time. Never encouraging them to do things, not really trying to interest them in anything, just trying to keep them quiet and still, and crush them into the right shape, so that they would go to university and 'do well.'"

Roger was considered to be more or less useless at most subjects, including English, "and the Art teacher was so ineffectual that he was practically not there at all." In fact there was a problem which the education authorities were trying to redress but which received little coverage in the press: many trained teachers had been killed in the war (such as Roger's father) and others had witnessed such horrors that their mental balance had been permanently affected. This resulted in a shortage of teachers that was dealt with both by bringing teachers out of retirement – who of course brought their old fashioned ideas about education with them – and by putting men back to work who in these more enlightened times would have received years of psychotherapy or counseling before being put in front of a roomful of children. Naturally the children knew nothing of this and made no allowances for the fact that most of their teachers had fought in the war.

Roger's reading of the situation, like many of his fellow pupils, was that most – not all – of these men were bitter and cynical. Roger told Ladd: "We had one guy who I would fantasise that his wife beat him. Certainly she treated him like shit and he was a really crushed person and he handed as much of that pain onto us as he could and he did quite a good job of it. And it's funny how those guys, when you get those guys at school, is they will always pick on the weakest kid as well. So the same kids who are susceptible to bullying by other kids are also susceptible to bullying by teachers as well. It's like smelling blood. They home in on fear and start hacking away – particularly with the younger children... Sarcasm. Sarcastic bastard."

The grammar schools had a cadet force to provide basic military training and to identify future officers and career military. Roger couldn't stand the itching of his khaki army uniform so he joined the Combined Cadet Force which led him to spend the occasional weekend at HMS Ganges, the naval training school which took boys as young as 14 and made them into naval seamen. At first Roger was absolutely horrified by it. He couldn't believe that children that young were being turned into cannon fodder. He also spent weekends on HMS Vanguard before she was scrapped but he didn't like life at sea because he was susceptible to seasickness. Nonetheless, despite his later blank dismissal of everything to do with the school, he enjoyed being in the sea cadets and became a leading seaman. Part of it was because he enjoyed firing guns; so much so that he used to shoot for the school in competition small bore shooting.

"I think there's something in me that makes me want to kind of dominate people anyway," he told Karl Dallas, "so I did all that in the cadet force and was, I think, roundly hated by most people involved. In fact, one weekend, I was set upon by a bunch of enraged schoolboys and dealt with." It sounds like a precursor of the attitudinal problems that were later to cause Roger to leave the Pink Floyd and for the band to continue without him. The cadets serving under his command gave him a good thrashing and according to Roger: "I learned a lesson then, a bit. It's not a terribly good thing to throw your weight around too much. And then I left... I still abuse it sometimes."

The school's only concern was to get their students into university; preferably into Oxbridge. Roger told Chris Salewicz: "It was a real battery farm. I hated it. All they would do was look at your most obvious aptitude and cram you into that pigeon-hole. I found physics and things like that quite easy to cope with and so I was pushed down that road." Roger had to stay on for a third year in the sixth form because he failed his pure maths A-level and became the only student in living memory who stayed on for a third year without being made a prefect, something he was rather proud of.

Roger clearly had a 'bad attitude'. "Toward the end when I was a teenager, going to school was just an 'us and them' confrontation between me and a few friends who formed a rather violent and revolutionary clique. That was alright, and I enjoyed the violence of smashing up the school property." The decision not to make him a prefect might also have had something to do with his dishonourable discharge from the Combined Cadet Force. He had suddenly decided that he no longer wanted to be a part of it. He couldn't resign, there were no provisions in the rules for people to leave, so he

'I think there's something in me that makes me want to kind of dominate people anyway'

Roger Waters

just handed his uniform back in and told them he wasn't going any more. His final school report said: "Waters never fulfilled his considerable potential and was dishonourably discharged from the cadet force." From the militarism of the naval cadets, Roger turned to the Campaign for Nuclear Disarmament (CND), and worked with Cambridge YCND (Youth Campaign for Nuclear Disarmament). He dealt with young people and students who were not at the university; college students were organised by the Combined Universities CND. He also became chairman of the Cambridge Young Socialists, though he later felt that all these activities were done more to please his mother rather than him holding strong views in these areas himself.

In case one is tempted to think that Roger Waters' assessment of his school was somewhat exaggerated, he is supported by an internet posting – unrelated to Pink Floyd – by an ex-High School boy Simon Knott who described "the sadism of a French master, who would wind his fingers into his victims' hair as he pressed their faces into the desk! On the door of another master's room the sign 'Arbeit Macht Frei': *Work Sets You Free*, the terrible lie once written above the entrance gates of the Auschwitz concentration camp!" Knott goes on to describe the arrogance of the masters, the sarcasm and the bullying: "Children never to be valued, never to be nurtured, never to be loved" but most of all, the interminable grim reality of wasted lives, year after year of boredom at a time when children are at their most receptive. No wonder Waters hated the place. It is fortunate that the school finally closed, to be reopened as the Hills Road Sixth Form College in 1974. However it has to be said that Syd Barrett, two years below Roger, seems to have sailed through it all, oblivious and unaware that he was living in a fascist regime.[*]

In interviews Waters always gave an unremittingly bleak assessment of the school and never recalled a single happy memory of his time there but it is well known that he enjoyed sports and presumably his friendships with many of the people later associated with Pink Floyd were forged, in part, because they were with him on the same teams: early Floyd member Bob Klose (real name Rado, but always known by the abbreviation of his second name) and future Pink Floyd art director Storm Thorgerson, the son of Mary Waters' closest friend, who were both in the year below Roger. Bob Klose, Storm Thorgerson and Roger were also on the County High cricket team together. To extend the Floyd connection: Roger's best friend at school was Andrew Rawlinson and a year above them was Geoff Mottlow, later a member of the Boston Crabs but who first had a band called Geoff Mott and the Mottoes featuring Syd Barrett on guitar. Rawlinson, Mottlow and Waters were together on the rugby team. In addition, Klose's family was good friends with David Gilmour's family.

When Roger left school he was all ready to study Mechanical Engineering at Manchester University but suddenly the thought came to him that he was facing three more years of study on a par with the same set of circumstances he had been under in the Sixth Form. He balked and took a year off to consider his options. Already displaying the self-confidence and independence that was to give him strength, and to cause him problems in the future with fellow band members, he began hitch-hiking around Britain at the age of 13 and as soon as he was old enough to drive, he got hold of a car and went around Europe. In the summer break of 1960, at the age of 17, he set out for Baghdad, exploring the Lebanon and roaming around the Middle East. Roger: "That was very much part of being in Cambridge at that time. We adopted the American literature of the period, things like *On The Road* by Kerouac, and the Beat poets like Gregory Corso and Ginsberg, and there was this idea of going East in search of adventure."

After taking a series of aptitude tests at the National Institute of Industrial Psychology they advised him that he would do well at architecture. He later realised that he was being completely passive in allowing these outside agencies to decide his fate, but at the time he went along with it and applied to the Regent Street Polytechnic's architecture department. But first he had to learn to draw because he needed a portfolio of drawings to show at the admissions interview. He began spending more time with Syd Barrett, going to gigs, riding around on his motorcycle, smoking pot and hanging out with girls. The circle of friends he had in Cambridge would remain central in his life: his first wife, two band members, the group's designers and even many of their roadies were all Cantabrigians.

[*]Others seemed more excited at the fact that the headmaster at the time, Mr. Brym Newton-John later moved to Australia with his daughter Olivia.

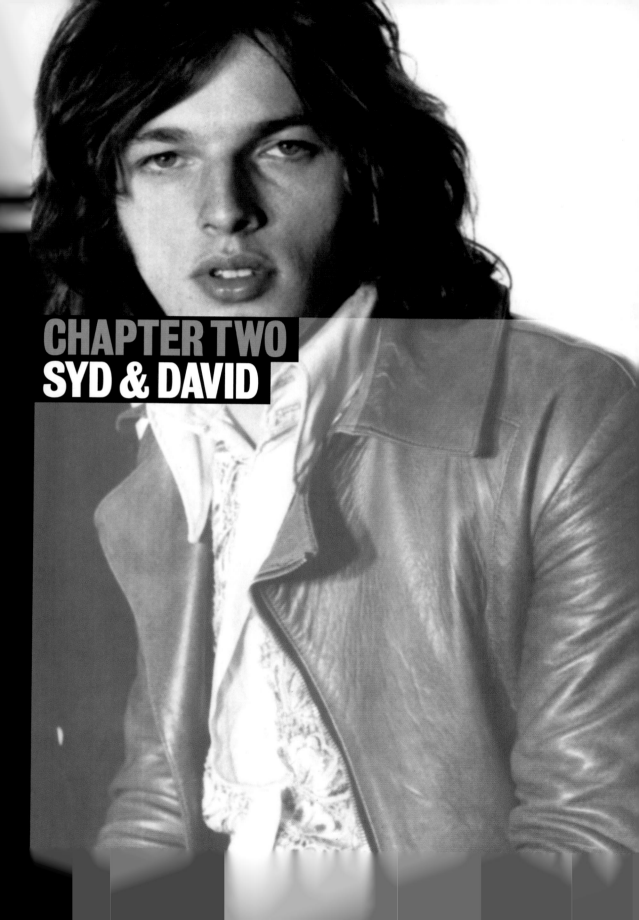

CHAPTER TWO
SYD & DAVID

CHAPTER TWO
SYD & DAVID

SYD BARRETT

Roger Keith Barrett was born January 6, 1946 at 60 Glisson Road,
off Hills Road, Cambridge, the fourth of five children: Alan (b. 1937),
Donald, Ruth and Rosemary. His father, Dr. Arthur Max Barrett had
attended Cambridge High School before making his career at the
London Hospital. It was at the London Hospital that he met
Winifred Flack who worked there as the head of the kitchens. She
came from a distinguished London family, her great grandmother,
Elizabeth Garrett Anderson, having been the first woman physician
in Great Britain. It was largely as a result of Anderson's
campaigning efforts that women were able to enter the medical
profession. A year after her death in 1917, her small dispensary was
named the Elizabeth Garrett Anderson Hospital in her honour.*

In 1938, Dr Barrett was appointed University Demonstrator in
Pathology at Addenbrooke's Hospital in Cambridge and he returned
to his home town with his wife – they were married in 1935 – to raise
a family. They quickly became central figures in the intellectual life
of Cambridge. Dr. Barrett loved music and was a member of the Cambridge
Philharmonic Society; there was an upright piano in the music room around which
the family would sometimes gather. He had his own key to the University Botanical
Gardens on Hills Road where he painted plants in watercolour. He was also an expert
on fungi and is said to have written several books on that subject though there is no
record of them at the British Library. There are suggestions that he illustrated them
himself, so Syd's artistic talent probably came from his father's side of the family. His
mother had a great interest in scouts and guides and was a high ranking figure in the
county Girl Guides Brigade. She did a lot of social work, running a lunch club for old-
age pensioners and doing other good works.

In 1950, when Syd was four, the family moved a few blocks south to a large double-
fronted, five bedroom house at 183 Hills Road, large enough for all the family and their
friends. Hills Road was a good deal more leafier then and had a lot less traffic. There
was a large, well lit, double-height entry hall with an open staircase which led to a
wooden first-floor gallery, protected by a wooden balustrade off which lay the
bedrooms. The kitchen and living room was always filled with visitors and the
childrens' schoolmates. It was a big, friendly household but when Dr. Barrett was
appointed the university's Morbid Anatomist – he worked as a police pathologist –
he was so occupied with his work at Addenbrooke's that he rarely was able to spend
time alone with any of his children. He engaged in a number of research programmes
including pioneer research into cot death syndrome and after his death a ward was
named after him.

Young Roger (to be referred to as Syd from now on to distinguish him from Roger
Waters) was a keen scout. It was a family tradition; his parents had first got together

*The Elizabeth Garrett Anderson
Hospital is now an important
part of the University of London
College Hospitals.

24

on a London Hospital scout troupe outing to Essex in the hot summer of 1930 when they encountered each other in a haystack. Syd enjoyed camping and outdoor activities and graduated from cub scout to scout and finally Boy Scout Patrol Leader. Syd was a gregarious, extrovert child; the clown of the family with a great sense of humour – he would entertain everyone by playing the Jew's harp, acting out Eccles and Major Bloodnok from *The Goon Show*, and imitating Wilfred Pickles' Yorkshire accent from the BBC quiz show *Have A Go* – but he was a spoiled child and used to getting his own way. As the youngest boy, his mother doted on him but when things didn't go as he planned he was capable of violence: breaking windows, throwing stones at passing cars and misbehaving until he once more gained control.

Syd and his younger sister, Rosemary ('Roe'), were closest in age and spent a great deal of time together, sharing a bedroom and becoming very close. They often went roller-skating together or explored Grantchester Meadows where they would bathe in the River Cam. The meadows remained one of Syd's favourite places and he attributed the strong atmosphere of childhood innocence in his lyrics, the references to fairy tales and nursery rhymes, to his idyllic childhood: "I think a lot of it has to do with living in Cambridge, with nature and everything – it's so clean, and I still drive back a lot. Maybe if I'd stayed at college I would have become a teacher." When Syd was seven, he and Rosemary won the piano prize at the Cambridge Guildhall for a rendition of 'The Blue Danube.'

At Hills Road he was enrolled in the Morley Memorial Junior School, being taught by Mary Waters, Roger's mother. He was so close to his sister that when it came time for her first day at the school, it was Syd that took Rosemary, not their mother. According to Roe they skipped down the road hand-in-hand together but according to Syd's teachers he was sometimes so reluctant to attend school that his father had to bring him. It was clear that with the obvious exception of art, Syd was not much good at his lessons and he only just scraped through the 11+ examination to Cambridge County High School, just up Hills Road from his house. Though he does not seem to have suffered in the same way as Roger at the County, Syd encountered disciplinary problems, particularly when he would arrive at school without his school blazer or tie. He had wide flat feet and felt more comfortable with no shoelaces and socks, something the school also frowned upon. He was hyperactive, always bouncing on the balls of his feet – a habit he continued into adulthood – and continually interrupted the teachers to excitedly make his own point, but whereas Roger reacted to the teachers with peevish ill-will, Syd had early on discovered that he could usually charm people into letting him have his own way. He was usually able to talk his way out of situations and would wheedle his way around the teachers with smiles and jokes. Syd won poetry reading and public speaking competitions and played the lead in school plays, all of which appealed to his extrovert side. According to his sister Rosemary, many of the twists and turns in Syd's songs that his fans took so seriously were really jokes, designed to put people on.

Syd's personality changed dramatically when his father died suddenly on December 11, 1961. Dr Barrett had developed an aggressive cancer and, though the children knew that he was ill, the seriousness of his condition was not made apparent until about a week before his death so it came as a great shock. Syd could not

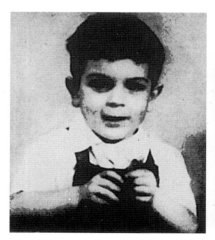
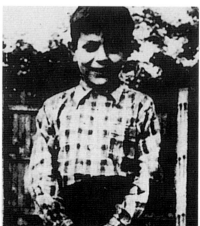

Opposite left & right: Syd Barrett as a child.

Above: The Madcap Laughs session, Earl's Court, 1969.

concentrate on his studies and he became rebellious and difficult at home, unable to deal with a situation where he had no control. His sister thinks that out of all the children, Syd was possibly most affected by their father's death. Winifred now had to bring up five children as a single mother and could no longer devote as much attention to him as before. Money was also a problem and she began to take in lodgers to supplement her income, two to each spare room. This was a common occurrence in the neighbourhood and the lodgers were all 'high class' people: among Winifred's guests were Junichiro Koizumi, later the prime minister of Japan, and Jean Moreau's daughter. The three older children had all left home so Syd was moved from his upstairs bedroom into the large ground floor to the left of the hall which was fitted with its own Yale lock, giving him in effect a bedsitter of his own.

Syd reacted very badly to all these changes. He threw himself into his art, spending as much time painting as possible. He more or less took over the big communal room downstairs as a painting studio and would often creep away from school to go home and paint; he only lived across the street. Cross-country running was a good lesson for him to sneak away from; he would start the run with the rest of the boys, drop back, then go home, get in an hour of painting, return to the route and join the run somewhere towards the end, huffing and puffing as if he had run the entire distance.

If art was his first love, music came a close second. Like most of his friends, Syd tuned in to Radio Luxembourg in the evenings for black American rock 'n' roll and rhythm 'n' blues: Bo Diddley was his favourite, and remained so. Luxembourg was also good for skiffle which caused Syd to take up the ukulele. His older brother, Alan, was also keen and played saxophone in a local skiffle group for a while. According to Floyd folklore, Syd's first real instrument was a banjo, given to him when he was 11 by his father. Syd later claimed that he found it in a second hand store and "plunked away quite happily for about six months. Then I decided to get a guitar." This suggests that he was older than 11 which appears more likely. His first guitar was a Number 12 Hofner Acoustic, bought by his parents when he was 14, which he played in his bedroom with friend John Gordon, using an amplifier that Syd made himself from a kit. Syd and John called themselves the Hollerin' Blues.

When he was 16 Syd joined a local group, Geoff Mott & the Mottoes and switched to

'On the train
remember si
making a dra
equipment v
ever need, w
of two Vox A

Roger Waters

a Futurama 2. "At the time I thought it was the end in guitars," said Barrett. "Fantastic design." It was an iconic instrument, an inexpensive copy of the Fender Stratocaster, with its cut-away body, its angled machine-head ending in a rounded phallic curve and of course its vibrato-bar which made for a whole new range of guitar hero histrionics even though it often threw the guitar out of tune. This was the big switch, musically, from Woody Guthrie, folk and blues, to the electric music of the Shadows.

Aside from Syd on guitar and vocals and Geoff Mott as lead singer, the lineup of Geoff Mott & the Mottoes consisted of Tony Sainty on bass and Clive Wellham on drums. They practiced in Syd's room on Sunday afternoons and, according to Syd, did a lot of work at private parties. However, Barrett scholars say there was only one proper gig, a local CND fundraiser – perhaps organised by Roger Waters who was at school with Geoff and played alongside him in the High School rugby team. As the chairman of YCND Cambridge, Roger sometimes designed posters for the group who mostly played Shadows instrumentals, plus a few Buddy Holly and Eddie Cochran songs, along with some original material. Roger occasionally sat in at band practice in Syd's room but he was not yet a proficient guitarist.

Roger had saved up enough money from pea-picking to buy a 1946 Francis Barnet 125cc motor cycle on which he roared around the Cambridge streets, an apparently terrifying sight with his long legs and teeth clenched tightly together. Roger: "Syd Barrett – who was a couple of years younger – and I became friends in Cambridge. We both had similar interests – rock 'n' roll, danger and sex and drugs, probably in that order. I had a motor bike before I left home, and we used to go on mad rides out into the country. We would have races at night, incredibly dangerous, which we survived somehow. Those days – 1959 to 1960 – were heady times."

Syd and Roger were part of a group of young people who hung out at the Criterion pub, a run-down establishment in Cambridge's town centre, where they kept company with Aubrey Powell – known as 'Po' – Storm Thorgerson and David Gilmour. Roger: "Syd and I went through our *most* formative years together, riding on my motorbike, getting drunk, doing a little dope, flirting with girls, all that basic stuff. I still consider Syd a great primary inspiration; there was a wonderful human tenderness to all his unique musical flights."

Being a university town there was a lot of interest in the American Beat Generation and like Roger, Syd was interested in the poetry of Allen Ginsberg and Gregory Corso and the novels of Jack Kerouac and William Burroughs; Syd was particularly fond of Kerouac's *On The Road*. Roger also read James Joyce though he was never a big reader: "There was a very strong pseudo-intellectual but beat vibe. It was just when the depression of the postwar was beginning to wear off and we were beginning to go into some kind of economic upgrade. And just at the beginning of the Sixties there was a real flirtation with prewar romanticism, which I got involved with in a way, and it was that feeling that pushed me toward being in a band."

Roger and Syd spent a lot of time listening to music together although Roger had still not yet learned to play well enough for them to jam properly. However it was understood between them, that Roger would go to London to study architecture and that Syd would eventually follow him to the capital to study art. Once there, they

me I clearly
g with Syd
g of all the
hought we'd
n consisted
s.'

would form a band together. This was confirmed on November 21, 1961, when Roger and Syd went up to London to see Gene Vincent at the Gaumont State Ballroom, Kilburn. Roger: "On the train home I clearly remember sitting with Syd making a drawing of all the equipment we thought we'd ever need, which consisted of two Vox AC30s."

Syd won an arts scholarship and in September 1962, he began a two year arts programme at the Cambridge College of Arts and Technology (CCAT) on Collier Road. Among his fellow students was his Cambridge musical friend John Gordon. Syd quickly adopted the correct art school beatnik look: he dropped the Brylcremed quiff and squeezed into tight black "drainies", bought a baggy sweater and shades to match those worn by Zbigniew Cybulski in Wajda's 1958 masterpiece *Ashes And Diamonds* that put an entire generation of would-be existentialists into dark glasses. His outfit was completed by a pair of grey moccasins or flapping laceless shoes. At college they called him 'Syd-the-Beat', after his interest in Beat Generation literature and his sartorial daring. Trad jazz was big with art students then and, like Roger, Syd took to hanging out at the Riverside Jazz Club at the Anchor on Mill Pond. There he got to know the house band whose drummer was called Sid Barrett. Syd was naturally given the same name, only spelt with a 'y'. Syd enjoyed his new name which was like the Goons' 'Sid-er-ney' and 'Sid-knee'.

His then girlfriend Libby Gausden , whose father taught at CCAT, complained to Tim Willis that she and Syd argued over presents: she wanted a 45 of Gerry & the Pacemakers' late-1964 hit 'Ferry Cross The Mersey' but instead he gave her *Red Bird*, a 1959 EP of Christopher Logue reading his poetry to jazz. It was typical of the direction he was going in. His painting changed from more figurative work to abstraction and he began to use collage elements such as lace on his canvases. Like most British art students at the time, he was influenced by the shows of American abstract expressionism and pop art put on at the Whitechapel Art Gallery, the Tate Gallery and the American Embassy where works by Pollock, de Kooning, Rauschenberg, Johns, Warhol and Rothko were exhibited. There was also a great interest in Kurt Schwitters 'Mertz' objects at this time and Tooth's were showing the collage work of Dubuffet. It was an exciting time in art and Syd followed it closely but as he was bored at college and would strum his Hofner with his bare toes beneath his desk.

In the summer of 1963, Syd joined an impromptu blues band called Those Without in which he played a Hofner bass, an instrument he used for several years. The other members were Alan Sizer on guitar and vocals, someone called "Smudge" on guitar and Steve Pyle on drums. The band continued with a changing line-up and Syd played with them again in January 1965, only this time as lead singer and guitarist.

In 1964, Syd and Steve Pyle from Those Without combined with members of David Gilmour's first group, the Newcomers (though without David) to play a few gigs under the revived name of the Hollerin' Blues. Ken Waterson was on vocals, harmonica and maracas, fellow Newcomer Barney Barnes was on keyboards, piano and vocals, and Pete Glass played harmonica. Like all of Syd's early bands, the Hollerin' Blues practiced in his bedroom at the Barrett family home where all were made welcome and a tea-trolley was left outside the door. As far as Winifred was concerned, Syd was a genius and everything he did was creative and special.

Another of Syd's friends from Cambridge was Seamus O'Connell, who had been two years above Gilmour at the Perse school. O'Connell's rather bohemian mother was separated from his father and encouraged Seamus to have his friends around, no doubt preferring them to be where she could keep an eye on them. Roger Waters was a regular visitor there and described how Seamus's mother would stay up all night, cooking boiled potatoes and sausages for Seamus and his friends while they listened to jazz and blues records. She had an interest in the occult and Syd spent hours browsing through her library of books on the Tarot, magic, astrology and the *I-Ching*, or *Book Of Changes*, asking her questions and following up her answers. He was absorbing ideas and images which would shortly come tumbling out as songs.

It was at CCAT that Syd and David Gilmour met again and became friends. Gilmour, whose nickname was "Fred", for much the same inexplicable reason that Roger's name became Syd, was a much more dedicated musician and it was through his friendship with David that Syd's interests focused more on music.

DAVID GILMOUR

David Jon Gilmour was born on March 6, 1946 at 109 Grantchester Meadows, across from the River Cam in Cambridge, the second of three sons to Sylvia and Douglas

Above (left): Pink Floyd, EMI House, 1967.

Above: Syd and Roger. Syd is holding his mirrored Fender Telecaster.

Below: 109
Grantchester
Meadows –
the childhood
home of David
Gilmour.

Gilmour. His father was a professor of genetics and a senior lecturer in zoology at the university and his mother was a teacher and later a film-editor on *Junior Points Of View*, the ITV programme which allowed younger viewers to give their opinion on television shows. David's parents appear to have been a bit bohemian, easy going, or even lax, depending how you look at it. He told Phil Sutcliffe: "They enjoyed each other's company and I think they found us rather inconvenient."

In 1951, when Douglas Gilmour took a one year job in America, David and his younger brother were put in a boarding school. David: "I was five and my brother was four! Which is pretty strange, isn't it? Later you think, 'Hang on, that wasn't so nice'." After the age of 10 David never accompanied them on holidays; when they went to France, he was sent off to Scout Camp which, fortunately, he enjoyed.

It was a musical family. David: "My parents sung well, my brother played flute, and my sister the violin." The first record David bought was Bill Haley's 'Rock Around The Clock' on a shellac 78 which, sadly, and to his acute distress, his parents' au pair girl sat on. His second was Elvis Presley's 'Jailhouse Rock'. During the blues and folk revival of the late Fifties/early Sixties David, like Roger and Syd, listened to a lot of Leadbelly, Sonny Terry and Brownie McGhee, and Howlin' Wolf. Like most early Sixties musicians, David couldn't help but be influenced by the Shadows and Hank Marvin, "hence the red Strat" – as he stated on his website – the guitar most associated with him from Floyd days.

But he began on a more humble instrument; when he was 13 David acquired a Tatay Spanish guitar, loaned to him by a friend next door. The boy's mother had given him the instrument but he was not very interested in it and David forgot to give it back. With the aid of Pete Seeger's tutor, he quickly learned to play: the first track taught how to tune the instrument and how to play a few chords. David never got beyond the third track but it got him started. He would sit up late at night, listening to Radio Luxembourg on headphones attempting to work out the bass, rhythm and lead guitar parts of every record that came on: "and try to learn all the parts of my favorite songs – bass, rhythm guitar, lead. Naturally it took a while, often involving 20 passes or more at the song during a week's time!"

"I spent a lot of time with friends," Gilmour told David Mead, "and Bob Klose, who was in the very early incarnation of Pink Floyd and was one of my childhood friends, he played a lot of blues music and stuff to me. My scale of interest was incredibly broad: folk music through blues and through to straight pop music. I wouldn't say blues was the dominant one."

109 Grantchester Meadows – the name of a road in the south part of Newnham, not in Grantchester itself – is in an idyllic English setting, one of a row of large houses situated on the edge of the meadows on the popular footpath and bicycle track sometimes known as the Grantchester Grind that follows the River Cam to Grantchester where it emerges at The Orchard, the outdoor tea garden popular with students ever since its opening in 1868 (the poet Rupert Brooke used to lodge there). The River Cam and the meadows are the source of the distant bells, summer evening birds, and holding hands by the river in David's song 'Fat Old Sun' on the (1970) Pink Floyd album, *Atom Heart Mother*.

David went to the Perse School, a common-entrance, fee-paying private school on Hills Road, originally founded as a grammar school back in 1615. Two years above him were Seamus O'Connell, David Gale (later Syd's flatmate in London), and film-maker Anthony Stern who, like Roger sporting friends, all formed parts of the link that joined the Floyd and their circle. Now, as when Gilmour attended, the Perse has some of the best academic results in the country, though David had some trouble with his modern language A-levels and in 1963 decided to go on to Cambridge College of Arts and Technology and retake them there. (He failed.)

Cambridge is not large, and most people of a certain age knew each other, relationships moved and changed between the boys and girls and a lot of time was spent sitting in El Patio or the Kenya Coffee House talking teenage dreams over frothy Pyrex cups of coffee. At CCAT David and Syd spent each lunch hour in a painting studio in the art department playing guitars together, studying R&B riffs and analysing Keith Richards' style. They would go to Millers Music Centre and try to memorise the riffs when listening to records in the booths.

"We sat around learning Beatles songs, Rolling Stones songs, R&B, blues songs..." Gilmour told Alan di Perna. "I can recall spending some time working on 'Come On', the first Stones A-side (June 1963), working all that out, playing harmonicas and stuff. He'd know something, I'd know something, and we'd just swap, as people do in back

'I can recall spending some time working on 'Come On', the first Stones A-side (June 1963), working all that out, playing harmonicas and stuff. He'd know something, I'd know something, and we'd just swap, as people do in back rooms everywhere.'

David Gilmour

rooms everywhere." By this time David had a Hofner Club 60, the best of the three Club models with its ebony fingerboard and inlay to the machine head and neck. This was the guitar that launched many Sixties British rockers, as photographs of the young John Lennon and Paul McCartney show.

David and Syd both owned the *Pete Seeger Teaches Guitar* self-tutoring guitar book and record set and would get together in Syd's room at 183 Hills Road to practice the chords. David told Karl Dallas: "We spent a lot of time together as teenagers listening to the same music. Our influences are pretty much the same. I don't want to go into print saying that I taught Syd Barrett everything he knows, 'cause its patently untrue, but there are one or two things in Syd's style that I know come from me." David became a regular visitor to 183 and was easily the better guitarist with a much greater technical mastery and was able to help Syd with a number of things. Syd was always more concerned with effects, textures and musical tricks than with expressing himself musically on the instrument. According to Bob Klose he could only play E and A-major, and strum a 12-bar blues: G7, C7, and D7. His skill lay much more with lyrical ideas. Sometimes Syd and David would take their guitars to the Mill, a riverside pub on Mill Lane by the Weir, and play an acoustic session together.

David's first band the Newcomers were in existence between January and October 1963. Originally called Chris Ian & the Newcomers, the band shortened their name to the Newcomers after Chris Ian Culpin, the drummer, left and was replaced by Willie Wilson in March. David was on guitar and vocals, and the rest of the band consisted of Johnny Philips and Ken Waterson on vocals, Roger Bibby on bass and Barney Barnes on rhythm guitar. They had two managers, David Hurst and Nigel Smith, so they probably did play some gigs. The Newcomers rehearsed in the scout hut on Perne Road, using a domestic hi-fi system including corner hi-fi speaker cabinets on three legs with a small amp in the back that would constantly fail. The units would hum and buzz and vibrate their way across the stage like miniature robots. (After the Newcomers disbanded early in 1964, Wilson and Waterson went on to join Syd in the Hollerin' Blues.)

In March 1962, Clive Welham, who had played drums with Syd in both the 1960 Hollerin' Blues trio and in Geoff Mott & the Mottoes, started his own band, the Ramblers, whose line-up consisted of Richard Baker on bass, John Gordon, the third member of the original Hollerin' Blues, on rhythm guitar, Chris 'Jim' Marriot and his brother Mervyn on vocals and Albert Prior on lead guitar. David sat in with the Ramblers during April and May 1963 and also played with them at Sawston Village College late that year.

A few months later, David, Clive Welham and John Gordon decided to reform the group under the name Joker's Wild. Completing the line up were multi-instrumentalist David Altham on guitar, saxophone, keyboards and vocals and Tony Sainty, the original bass player with Geoff Mott & the Mottoes. They practiced at David's parents' house on Grantchester Meadows and had a residency every Wednesday at the Victoria Ballroom* in the Market Square in the centre of Cambridge from 1964 until 1966 and often played the nearby US Air Force bases at Lakenheath and Mildenhall as well as the usual pubs and parties. David: "We were quite popular because we played all the current dance music, and that's what people wanted to hear. At one point, we had five residencies at the same time."

All five men were vocalists so their repertoire tended toward high harmony material as performed by the Beatles, Beach Boys, Four Seasons and countless black American R&B groups like the Coasters or the Wrens. An acetate exists of their cover versions of Frankie Lymon & the Teenagers' 1956 doo-wop hit 'Why Do Falls Fall In Love?' and conversely, Manfred Mann's R&B-styled 'Don't Ask Me What I Say' (from their 1964 debut album *The Five Faces Of Manfred Mann*).

In the summer of 1965, Syd and Storm Thorgerson drove down to the south of France in a beat up Land Rover. David, whose parents were once more in America, hitch-hiked down and met up with them in a camp site near St. Tropez. David: "Bacon and eggs on the Primus for breakfast - fantastic." They busked on the streets for change, playing Beatles numbers from the Fabs' new film *Help!* until French police arrested them for not having a permit. It was not until the ill-fated five-piece Pink Floyd line-up that David and Syd again played together in a band.

On the way back the trio stopped off in Paris and bought the green paperback Olympia Press Travellers Companion books that were banned in England such as *The Naked Lunch* by William Burroughs, and Pauline Reagé's *The Story of O*. "I remember sitting in the campsite reading these things," Gilmour recalls.

Right: Joker's Wild,
David's pre-Floyd
Cambridge group.
David on left.

Back in Cambridge, David and Syd, in the spirit of the times, fully experimented with magic mushrooms – easily available in the meadows around town – hashish, easily available from certain pubs, and LSD which made an early appearance at both Oxford and Cambridge, thanks to certain professors bringing the formula back from Stamford University. "There was a seriousness to acid then, and even to dope," Gilmour told Tim Willis. "We wanted to explore the subconscious reaches of the mind, untap its potential. We were trying to understand the universe." There was, of course, a certain euphoria attendant to the experience as well. They were part of the same set of closely linked friends, to the extent that when Syd broke up with Vivien Brans in 1965, she next stepped out with David.

As well as lead guitarist in Joker's Wild, Gilmour was often the featured vocalist; Wilson Pickett's current hit, 'In The Midnight Hour' was his big number, augmented by a tricky solo on his flame timber Hofner Club 60 that made all the girls gasp in admiration. The band was organised in a very democratic way and was extremely professional considering they were all teenagers. Drummer Clive Werlham told Nicholas Schaffner that David's greatest musical asset was his sense of feel and timing: "What he does in a number is 99 % of the time *right*, and I used to love his guitar playing for that. Short riffs or whatever, whether he's playing a raunchy up-tempo number or something mellow and laid-back, it was always perfect for what was needed to be there. That's some intuition."

Meanwhile David's parents had moved to Greenwich Village, New York, where David's father had joined the so-called brain drain. In the late Fifties and early Sixties, hundreds of Britain's top scientists moved to the USA where salaries were astronomically higher and the labs were lavishly equipped. Rather than interrupt his education, David's easy going, liberal parents set the 18-year old up in a small flat on Mill Road near the centre of Cambridge and trusted him to get on without their parental guidance. He lived a typically bohemian life, getting in at 4 am after a gig, doing any jobs that came his way to supplement his income including working as a male model; presumably at the local art school. It was little wonder he failed his modern languages exams.

In 1966 David's brother Peter Gilmour* replaced Tony Sainty on bass in Joker's Wild who, by now, had developed a substantial local following. They opened for visiting acts such as Zoot Money's Big Roll Band and the Animals at places like the Dorothy Ballroom – 'the Dot' – where the Pink Floyd played in 1967 or the Rex where they played during their first major UK tour in 1969. But London was the place to make it. It was only 50 miles away and more and more this became the destination of the band's Ford Transit.

*The building is now a part of the Marks & Spencers chain.
*David's other brother Mark was a guitarist with Sixties group The Act.

CHAPTER THREE
THE MOVE TO TOWN

CHAPTER THREE
THE MOVE TO TOWN

Roger Waters succeeded in his application to join the Regent Street
Polytechnic's architecture department and in the summer of 1962
he moved to London. The main college building is on the west side
of upper Regent Street but the architecture school was housed in the
rather grand annex on nearby Little Titchfield Street complete with
St. George and the Dragon over the grand entrance. By this time
Roger had a few months work experience in an architectural office
and arrived full of self-confidence. He had an ambivalent attitude
toward his studies and years later, he unequivocally stated: "I've
never been interested in architecture." For whatever reason, he was
a poor scholar and after two years he was asked to leave for refusing
to attend his History of Architecture lectures.

As with secondary school, Roger blamed his problems with
authority on the teachers. "I was very bolshie," he told Chris
Salewicz. "I must have been horrible to teach. But the history
lecturer that I came up against was very reactionary, so it was a fair
battle. I said I wouldn't do exams because the guy refused to talk
to me. He'd tell us to sit down and copy a drawing off a blackboard. And I asked him
if he could explain why, because I couldn't see the point in copying something off a
blackboard that he was copying off a textbook. It was just like school. I couldn't handle
it. I'd hoped I'd escaped all that. When you go to university, you expect to be treated
like little grown-ups."

The practice of the teacher drawing floor plans for the students to copy was a
traditional one in architecture and had been practiced at the Poly ever since the place
was founded. Roger's reaction against outmoded tradition was predictable and
expected Sixties behaviour; it characterised the decade but Roger's method of dealing
with the situation was not very constructive. By all accounts he had an arrogant
attitude and went about with what Nick Mason in his autobiography described as
"an expression of scorn for most of the rest of us, which I think even the staff found
off-putting."

Roger first bought a guitar in Cambridge when he was 14, but he gave it up because
it was too difficult to learn: "It hurt my fingers, and I found it much too hard. I couldn't
handle it." He was able, however, to bang out 'Shanty Town' to anyone who cared to
listen. At the Poly his interest in playing was renewed. Roger: "I invested some of my
grant in a Spanish guitar and I went and had two lessons at the Spanish Guitar Centre
but I couldn't do with all that practice." Using Letraset, a peel-off lettering system
used by architects and graphic artists, he had written 'I believe to my soul' in neat
letters (almost certainly gil sans) across the sound board of his shiny new guitar and
presumably varnished it or else it would have rubbed off.

Roger: "The encouragement to play my guitar came from a man who was head
of my first year at architecture school at Regent Street Polytechnic, in London. He

encouraged me to bring the guitar into the classroom. If I wanted to sit in the corner and play guitar during periods that were set aside for design work and architecture, he thought that was perfectly alright. It was my first feeling of encouragement." With his new musical confidence he gravitated towards a group of students who wanted to form a band; as in most colleges there is always a room where people meet to play instruments, at the Poly it was the Student Players office where the Poly Drama Club rehearsed. Roger: "At the Polytechnic I got involved with people who played in bands, although I couldn't play very well. I sang a little and played the harmonica and guitar a bit."

His first 'professional' (i.e. semi-public) gig is listed as playing with fellow student Keith Noble as the Tailboard Two in the assembly hall of the Regent Street Polytechnic School. The name suggests a possible folk or country and western influence on the duo at the time which is intriguing. Though he was working in the same studio as both Rick Wright and Nick Mason, they had been in the same class for about six months, until the spring of 1963, before he got to know them.

RICK WRIGHT

Richard William Wright was born on July 28, 1943 to Cedric and Bridie Wright, in Hatch End, the most exclusive end of well-to-do Pinner, one of the 10 hamlets of the medieval Harrow Manor, in what was once rural Middlesex. Cedric was the chief biochemist for Unigate Dairies which enabled them to live comfortably in what had become a pleasant distant suburb of London. Rick's mother, Bridie, was originally from Wales and he had two sisters, Selina and Guinivere. He was sent first to St. John's School, an independent day prep school founded in 1920 in Pinner.*

It was a boys school of the traditional type; one of Wright's contemporaries there remembers being beaten virtually every day for minor infractions by vicious cane wielding masters. At 13 Rick took the common entrance exam and went as a day boy to the Haberdasher's Aske's Grammar School, then in Hampstead. The school has occupied many sites since it was founded in 1690 but though it was a direct grant grammar school, it maintained a certain formality: for instance many of the boys wore straw boaters in the summer. Rick was always musical; playing piano and trumpet when very young and at 12 years old he picked up the guitar when he was bedridden for two months with a broken leg. He learned to play without the aid of a tutor, in the manner of the old blues singers, and so used his own fingering and tuning. With the rise of trad jazz in the late Fifties he learned to play both trombone and saxophone and jammed with friends.

Rick was first attracted to classical music but then he encountered jazz on the radio; thanks to the combined efforts of the Musicians Union and the BBC this was white British jazz but interesting enough. He saw Humphrey Lyttelton and Kenny Ball play Eel Pie Island and was present when Cyril Davies introduced R&B to the Railway Tavern in Harrow. Then he discovered Miles Davis.

Wright told Q magazine that his all time favourite record was Miles Davis's *Porgy And Bess*: "*Porgy And Bess* is a brilliant record – the nearest thing to hearing a trumpet being made to sound like the human voice. I have to put this record on from beginning to end, because it stops you dead in your tracks. People might be surprised to hear me being so infatuated with jazz, but the influences in the Floyd came from lots of different areas. Syd was more into Bo Diddley; I had the more classical approach. If I was forced to pick an all-time favourite record, this would probably be it." Rick stated that he could easily list Miles Davis albums as his 10 favourite records. This positions him alongside many of his generation, including the author of this book, who eagerly awaited the new releases on the Blue Note, Impulse and Riverside labels by John Coltrane, Eric Dolphy, Horace Silver, Art Blakey's Jazz Messengers, Art Pepper and all the great albums released in the late Fifties and early Sixties. Nor was it impossible to detect references to Ornette Coleman, Cecil Taylor or even Albert Ayler in Rick's wilder moments at UFO, or so I imagined.

Rick did a stint as a delivery man for Kodak, presumably as a summer job, before going to the Poly in September 1962.

NICK MASON

Nick Mason also joined the Poly architectural school that year. He, at least, expected to graduate and become an architect even though his real interest was in cars. Nicholas Berkeley Mason was born in Edgbaston, a suburb of Birmingham, on January 27, 1944, to Bill and Sally Mason. He had three sisters Sarah, Melanie and

*It moved to nearby Northwood in 1970.

Serena. When Nick was two years old, his father was offered a job with the Shell Oil film unit and the family moved to Downshire Hill, Hampstead, a beautiful street filled with mainly Regency houses that lent its name to a school of artists, including Stanley Spencer and Mark Gitler, who gathered at number 47 between the wars. Running off it is Keats Grove where Keats lived and wrote 'Ode To A Nightingale' and at the north end is the Heath itself.

Bill Mason made films about motor sports and used to race himself. Nick first attended a motor race when he was six or seven and has been obsessed with the sport ever since. His father had joined the Communist Party in the Thirties as a way of opposing the growth of fascism and with the outbreak of war he resigned from the party to become a shop steward at the ACT, the Association of Cinematographic Technicians. Both Nick's parents were staunch Labour Party supporters which was one of the reasons he got on so well with Roger Waters whose mother was also an ex-Communist party member turned Labour Party activist.

Nick began drumming early on, having been given a drum set for Christmas when he was 13 years old after failing both violin and piano lessons. He used it to play in the school Dixieland jazz band. Like other members of the Floyd, and most of his generation in Britain, Nick stayed awake listening to Radio Luxembourg through the waves of static and bought Bill Haley's 'See You Later Alligator' on a fragile 78. He says that not only was Elvis Presley's 1956 *Rock 'N' Roll* his first LP but it was the first LP bought by two other members of Pink Floyd. The cover now has iconic status with Elvis strumming hard on his acoustic, eyes closed, bellowing away and his name spelled out in green and pink. It summed up everything rock 'n' roll was supposed to be about: youth, energy, sex; no wonder it was affectionately copied by the Clash for their 1979 album *London Calling*.

Nick soon found other boys in the neighbourhood who were interested in rock 'n' roll and by Christmas 1956 he found himself drumming as a member of the Hotrods, a combo featuring Tim Mack on lead guitar, William Gammell on rhythm, Michael Kriesky on bass and John Gregory on saxophone. Sadly their equipment was so

Right: Pink Floyd loon about outside EMI House, celebrating signing with the Beatles' label.

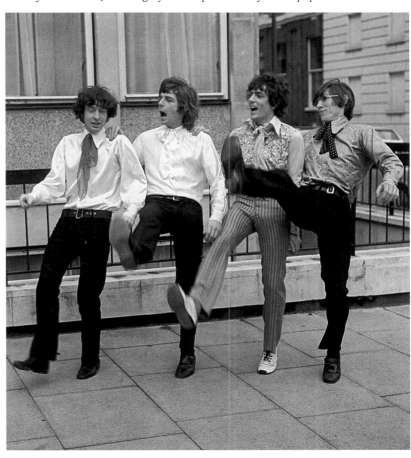

QUEEN ELIZABETH HALL, LONDON
PINK FLOYD REHEARSALS

This spread: Pink Floyd rehearsing at Queen Elizabeth Hall, London for the Games For May event, May 1967, which utilised the first full-scale use of stage props.

Right: Pink Floyd
promoting
'See Emily Play'
during one of
three consecutive
appearances on
BBC TV's Top Of
The Pops in 1967.

embarrassing that for their group photograph they had to mock up a Vox cabinet by drawing knobs on a cardboard box with a Biro. Musically, Mason wrote, they did little more than use Nick's father's Grundig tape recorder to record endless versions of Duane Eddy's summer 1959 hit version of Henry Mancini's 'The Peter Gunn Theme', a television detective series from the late Fifties.

After prep school, Nick was sent to board at Frensham Heights, a private co-educational school housed in a magnificent Edwardian country mansion near Farnham in Surrey. The school was set up in the Twenties in the liberal tradition and, though it was very academic, it also encouraged individual thought. It was there that Nick met his first wife, Lindy, who came from a similar left-wing background to himself. He enjoyed boating on Frensham ponds in his own canoe, dancing in the grand ballroom of the country house – foxtrots, waltzes, veletas – and later, even hops to pop music. There was only one record player in the school so the jazz club was somewhat restricted in its activities. After a year in London "improving my studies" and attending traditional jazz clubs like Ken Colyer's and the 100 Club, he entered the Regent Street Poly in September 1962. Nick enthusiastically embraced the student life, wearing corduroy jackets and a duffle coat with bone toggles; he even tried smoking a pipe.

Roger and Keith Noble decided to enlarge the Tailgate Two to be a proper group. Guitarist Clive Metcalfe, another Poly architecture student, had also been dueting with Keith Noble (perhaps also as the Tailgate Two?) and Metcalfe, Waters and Noble now invited Nick to join them in a new ensemble to be known as Sigma 6. The other members, necessary to make it Sigma 6 not the Sigma 4, were Keith Noble's sister Sheila who sometimes helped out on vocals, and Rick Wright on keyboards. Rick's situation was difficult because he did not possess an electric keyboard and was therefore only able to enhance the lineup when a pub happened to have a stand-up piano somewhere near the stage, though, as Nick pointed out, no-one could hear him over the Vox AC30s and drums without amplification anyway.

They were sometimes augmented by Rick's girlfriend, and later wife, Juliette Gale on vocals who was taking Modern Languages at the Poly. She specialised in blues standards such as 'Summertime' and 'Careless Love' and was apparently very good but she left at the end of their first year – the summer of 1963 – to study at the newly built University of Sussex in Brighton. At the same time Rick switched his studies from architecture to music and transferred to the London College of Music but by now he was an integral part of the group and continued to play with Sigma 6. He had quickly found that architecture was not his metier so, in addition to rehearsing and continuing with his architectural studies, he took a crammer course in order to enter the London College of Music. Rick: "I went to a private school, a dreadful private school, to do theory and composition. That was while I was going to architectural school as well, and after that I went to the London College of Music. Someone used to stand there, and he obviously didn't beat my hands if I went wrong, but it was a bit of a joke. I used to learn pieces off by heart, and then play them and pretend I was sight-reading, and of course, he caught me out. He said, 'Right, stop, and go back four bars.' And I didn't know where I was."

Vernon Thompson, a guitarist who could actually play his instrument, joined Sigma 6 briefly but left after a couple of rehearsals, taking his much admired Vox amplifier with him. The few gigs they played were usually for friends: private parties, student dances and the like. This was the time they were experimenting with names, among them the Abdabs, the Screaming Abdabs (in slang, to have a screaming abdab was to have an angry fit and lose control) and the Spectrum Five.

It was as the Abdabs that they gave their first ever interview, to Barbara Walters, writing in the Poly magazine:

"An up-and-coming pop group here at the Poly call themselves 'The Abdabs' and hope to establish themselves playing Rhythm and Blues. Most of them are architectural students. Their names are Nick Mason (drums); Rick Wright (rhythm guitar); Clive Metcalfe (bass); Roger Waters (lead); and finally Keith Noble and Juliette Gale (singers).

Why is it that Rhythm and Blues has suddenly come into its own? Roger was the first to answer.

'It is easier to express yourself rhythmically in Blues-style. It doesn't need practice, just basic understanding.' 'I prefer to play it because it is musically more interesting,' said Clive. I suppose he was comparing it to Rock. Well how does it compare? Roger was quite emphatic on this point. 'Rock is just beat without expression though admittedly Rhythm and Blues forms the basis of original Rock.'

It so happens that they are all jazz enthusiasts.

Was there any similarity? I asked.

In Keith's opinion there was.

'The Blues is just a primitive form of Modern Jazz.'

It is interesting to learn that Roger was still playing guitar at this point and Rick was also playing guitar in the absence of a keyboard. Most of their time was spent rehearsing in the tearoom in the basement of the Poly. In addition to a dozen or so R&B numbers such as John Lee Hooker's 'Crawling King Snake' they played the Searchers' 1963 hit, 'Sweets For My Sweet', and rehearsed songs written by a friend of Clive Metcalfe, a fellow Poly student called Ken Chapman. Chapman became quite involved with the group, becoming their informal manager and handing out printed cards offering their services, without much luck. His concern was mostly in having a band to play his songs, about which Nick Mason in his autobiography is polite but describes as 'a little too far on the ballad-cum-novelty side for us'. They did their best to help him but when the numbers were finally performed before music publisher Gerry Bron he was less than impressed. He didn't like the songs and he liked the band even less. Bron passed and instead started his own Bronze label, managing Manfred Mann, Uriah Heep and Collosseum in order to make his fortune. Shortly after this unsuccessful audition came the long summer break of 1963, after which Keith Noble and Clive Metcalfe left to form their own duo and with Juliette at university in Brighton, she was unable to sing with the group on a regular basis.

While Nick had sensibly, remained in the luxury of his parents' home, Roger was living just off the Kings Road in a rough flat with no telephone – usual for those days – and no hot water; he used the public Chelsea bathhouse just up the road. Nick would sometimes travel across London to join him at one of his local hang-outs, the Café des Artistes, a basement rock and roll club at 266a Fulham Road, where the Rolling Stones and other young bands gathered and where, in 1965, an embryonic Status Quo had their first residency. Now the two of them decided to share a flat together.

With two of the best musicians gone, Roger, Nick and Rick reformed around Roger

'One day I met a guy called Roger Waters who suggested that when I come up to a London Art School we got together and formed a group.'

Syd Barrett

and Nick's landlord, Mike Leonard. Leonard taught at Hornsey College of Art where, in 1962, he had set up their Sound and Light department to experiment with light projections and light machines. Roger and Nick knew him because he was also a part-time art tutor at the Poly. In September 1963 he bought a large high-ceilinged Edwardian house at 39 Stanhope Gardens in Highgate which he set about converting into a ground-floor flat with his own accommodation and art studio above. To help defray his mortgage he rented the newly converted flat to his students. Roger and Nick shared the ground floor front room, which also doubled as their rehearsal room. As they had their equipment permanently set up there it left no room for drawing boards so any architectural study was made doubly difficult.

The neighbours complained, but rather than make his tenants keep the noise down, Leonard joined in himself on piano, even buying a Farfisa Duo electric organ in order to become their keyboard player and for a period the band was known as Leonard's Lodgers. Leonard's interest was in finding experimental music that would go with his experiments with light. Mike Leonard's knowledge of lighting was of great use, but they had few occasions to call on his expertise for live gigs. Roger, however, developed a great interest in Leonard's light machines and spent many hours working with him at Hornsey College Light and Sound lab. Sometimes, when they felt in need of a protracted rehearsal, they gave the neighbours a break and rented a room in the Railway Tavern in nearby Archway Road. Nick Mason: 'Mike thought of himself as one of the band. But we didn't, because he was too old basically. We used to leave the house to play gigs secretly without telling him.' The year passed with few gigs, a lot of rehearsals and plenty of talk about the future.

In September 1964, two friends of Roger's from Cambridge, Syd Barrett and Bob Klose, moved to London. Klose went to the Poly and Syd to Camberwell Art College to do painting. Roger: 'They came to live in a flat in Highgate that I was living in. Nick Mason and Rick Wright had lived in it before us. With the advent of Bob Klose we actually had someone who could play an instrument. It was really then we did the shuffle job of who played what. I was demoted from lead guitar to rhythm guitar and finally bass. There was always this frightful fear that I could land up as the drummer.' To this latter task Nick Mason thankfully responded now that Roger had found his role as a bass player, otherwise he would have finished up as the roadie. In the same interview Waters was talking about a slightly later period regarding the living arrangements: Nick moved back to his parents' house that summer in order to concentrate on his studies as it was impossible to get any work done in the ground floor flat he shared with Roger. Bob Klose moved in to take his place. Roger's demotion to bass came about because he refused to use his grant money to buy an electric guitar.

Now all the Abdabs lacked was a vocalist. Bob Klose suggested a friend of his, Chris Dennis, a former member of the Cambridge band the Redcaps who was now serving as a dental assistant in the RAF, stationed at Northolt in London's western suburbs. Not only could he sing, but he owned a Vox PA system. Nick Mason is very amusing about Dennis in *Inside Out*, in particular his penchant for introducing numbers as 'Looking Through The Knotholes In Granny's Wooden Leg' and making Hitler moustaches with his harmonica. He was older than the others and had been badly affected by *The Goon Show*. The band name now alternated between the Abdabs and the Tea Set though the latter, had they kept it, would have inevitably caused problems as the British Tea Board advertised their wares at the time in a series of advertisements calling for the public to 'Join The Tea Set' featuring a gormless collection of happy tea drinkers, smiling at the camera with their little fingers crooked.

ENTER SYD

On November 6, 1963, Syd made a great sacrifice and missed seeing the Beatles play the Regal Theatre in Cambridge in order to attend his interview at Camberwell College of Art for which he borrowed a pair of shoes – with laces – from his girlfriend's father. Syd's shoes were always a subject of some amusement to the other members of the band. Roger Waters told John Ladd: 'Syd used to have elastic bands around his boots

Above: Syd Barrett was responsible for writing the Floyd's two UK hit singles and the bulk of their first album, The Piper At The Gates Of Dawn.

'cause the zippers were always breaking and you couldn't get the buttons done up.' Roger even referred to it in his song 'Comfortably Numb'.

Syd was offered a place at Camberwell starting at the end of September, 1964. That summer, David Gilmour's friend from the Perse, Seamus O'Connell moved with his mother to London where she rented a cheap flat in Tottenham Street, just off Tottenham Court Road. At the end of the block was Schmidt's, the magnificent, huge and cheap German restaurant on Charlotte Street, famous for the rudeness of its waiters, and at the other end was a bomb site on Whitfield Street; London was still rebuilding from the war. It was a perfect central location in what had, before the war, been the bohemian area of Fitzrovia. When Syd and his friend David Gale arrived in town they managed to find a bedsit in the same block. Gale had gone up to Cambridge University but took a year off to enjoy himself in London. He took a job at Better Books, on the Charing Cross Road where one of his colleagues was Adam Ritchie, who later took some of the most evocative photographs of the Pink Floyd at the UFO Club. Syd and Gale's bedsit was in an apparently terrifying building filled with drunken Irish navvies who filled the night with screams and the sound of breaking glass. It didn't suit Syd and not long after arriving, he moved out and joined Roger Waters and Bob Klose at Mike Leonard's house, sharing a room with Roger Waters while Bob Klose shared the other room with another Cambridge associate Dave Gilbert.

Roger: 'Syd and I had always vowed that when he came up to art school, which he inevitably would do being a very good painter, he and I would start a band in London. In fact, I was already in a band, so he joined that.' He did not join it immediately. Syd's priority was painting and it took a while for him to settle into art college routine. He came along to see the Abdabs rehearse. Mike Leonard had opened out the roof space of 39 Stanhope Gardens into an area that was perfect for rehearsals if you didn't mind humping all the equipment up stairs. They were playing there when Syd arrived late to watch. Afterwards he said, "Yeah, it sounded great, but I don't see what I would do in the band."

After Chris Dennis had returned to his RAF base a band meeting was held where it was decided that Dennis should go and Syd should join in his stead. As Bob Klose had hired the singer it naturally fell to him to break the news. He called Dennis from a pay phone in Tottenham Court Road but as it turned out Dennis was being posted abroad and would have had to resign anyway. And so Syd joined the band. As he once described it, in his oblique way: "One day I met a guy called Roger Waters who suggested that when I come up to a London Art School we got together and formed a group. This I did, and became a member of the Abdabs. I had to buy another guitar because Roger played bass, a Rickenbacker, and we didn't want a group with two bass players."

Rick Wright: "It was great when Syd joined. Before him we'd play the R&B classics, because that's what all groups were supposed to be doing then. But I never liked R&B very much. I was actually more of a jazz fan. With Syd, the direction changed, it became more improvised around the guitar and keyboards. Roger started to play the bass as a lead instrument and I started to introduce more of my classical feel."

Syd: "Their choice of material was always very much to do with what they were thinking as architecture students. Rather unexciting people, I would've thought, primarily. I mean, anybody walking into an art school like that would've been tricked – maybe they were working their entry into an art school. But the choice of material was restricted, I suppose, by the fact that both Roger and I wrote different things. We wrote our own songs, played our own music. They were older, by about two years, I think. I was 18 or 19. I don't know that there was really much conflict, except that perhaps the way we started to play wasn't as impressive as it was to us, even, wasn't as full of impact as it might've been. I mean, it was done very well, rather than considerably exciting. One thinks of it all as a dream."

By this time – 1964 – Syd and Roger had both begun their careers as lyricists. Syd had already written such numbers as 'Butterfly' and 'Remember Me' as well as 'Let's Roll Another One' (eventually released as 'Candy And A Currant Bun' on the B-side to 'Arnold Layne') which showed his early enthusiasm for pot (the words had to be changed before EMI would release it). Roger had written a song, generally thought to be his first ever song, called 'Walk With Me, Sydney', inspired by Syd's new name, and a pastiche of 'Work With Me, Henry' by Hank Ballard and the Midnighters (1954) that they would have known from studying old R&B records. It was designed to be sung by Syd and Juliette Gale:

Juliette: 'Ooooh, walk with me, Sydney.'

Syd: 'I'd love to, love to, love to, baby, you know.'
Juliette: 'Ooooh, walk with me, Sydney.'
Syd: 'I'd love to, love to, love to...'
Juliette: 'Ooh Sydney, it's a dark night./Hold me, hold me, hold me, hold me, hold me, hold me tight.'
Syd: 'I'd love to, love to, love to/But I've got flat feet and fallen arches, baggy knees and a broken frame/meningitis, peritonitis, DTs and a washed-out brain.'

This was the sort of light-hearted song they would play when they sang on the tube trains to raise money for Student Rag Week. With Syd on board, the line-up was now close to what was to become the Pink Floyd. Though it could easily have not happened. According to Tim Willis, Syd wrote to his then girlfriend Libby Gausden in Cambridge, reporting that a mutual friend had heard him rehearse with the Tea Set and told him that he should give it up because he sounded horrible. Syd told her: "He's right, and I would, but I can't get Fred to join because he's got a group. So I still have to sing." This letter is an extraordinary find because Fred was the Cambridge nickname for David Gilmour. This makes his replacement for Syd in the Pink Floyd something that they must have first been talking about as far back as 1964. But Syd persevered.

In October 1967 he told *Beat Instrumental*: "I changed guitars, and we started doing the pub scene.... A couple of months ago, I splashed out a couple of hundred on a new guitar, but I still seem to use that first one (a Fender Esquire Telecaster). It's been painted several times, and once I even covered it in plastic sheeting and silver discs. Those discs are still on the guitar, but they tend to look a bit worn. I haven't changed anything on it, except that I occasionally adjust the pickups when I need a different sound."

Like most colleges, the Poly student union put on regular concerts and dances in the large assembly hall. The dances were usually to records, but sometimes a band would be hired. On these occasions, as the only house band, the Tea Set got to play support. In this way they got to study the mechanics of putting on a professional show: stagecraft, setting up, tuning, loading gear and the rest. They played support to the Tridents, who featured Jeff Beck on guitar, then about to replace Eric Clapton in the Yardbirds. It was in the autumn of 1964 that they finally took the name Pink Floyd, though this was alternated with the Tea Set for many months to come whenever the Pink Floyd was deemed too freaky. The occasion was a gig at the RAF base at Uxbridge where they turned up only to find that the other band on the bill was also called the Tea Set. A new name was clearly in order and it was Syd who provided it.

Syd had two cats, one called Pink, after Pink Anderson, the blues singer from Laurens, South Carolina, who made three albums for Bluesville, and the other called Floyd, after Floyd Council from Chapel Hill, North Carolina. He played on several Blind Boy Fuller albums which is how Syd must have known of his work. Syd quickly joined together the names of his cats and produced the name Pink Floyd, though at first they called themselves the Pink Floyd Blues Band. Syd: "During that period we kept changing the name until we ended up with the Pink Floyd. I'm not sure who suggested it or why, but it stuck."

During the Christmas break they were able to make their first studio recording. Rick had a friend who worked in a recording studio in West Hampstead who let them use some unbooked studio time without charge. They cut Slim Harpo (James Moore)'s[*] 'I'm A King Bee' and three of Syd's compositions: 'Double O Bo' – described by Nick as 'Bo Diddley meets the 007 theme' – 'Butterfly' and 'Lucy Leave'.[*] They pressed up a limited number on acetates but usually sent out reel-to-reel tape copies (the Phillips cassette recorder did not come on the market until 1964 and was not yet in wide use) to prospective venues. It was also at this time that Rick sold his first song, receiving a £75 advance against royalties for 'You're The Reason Why' which appeared on the B-side of a 1964 Decca single, 'Little Baby' by Adam, Mike and Tim, a Liverpudlian folk-pop harmony group. Sadly, it bombed.

In the spring of 1965 they played their first residency; at the Countdown Club in the basement of 1A Palace Gate off Kensington High Street. Each Friday night they performed three 90 minute sets, beginning at 9 pm and ending at two in the morning[*] for a fee of £15. Playing such long sets meant that, in addition to learning a lot of new numbers, they quickly realised that the time could also be filled by long improvised solos. Although the band had about 80 songs in their repertoire – a mixture of R&B, Bo Diddley and Rolling Stones numbers – Nick remembers only two items from their set: a novelty number, 'Long Tall Texan' (originally recorded by Jerry Woodard and recently covered by the Beach Boys on their 1964 *Concert* album) and Bob Klose's

The Pink Floyd were hard to see because of their light show, which meant that even when they were famous they were rarely bothered by fans on the street.

showcase, 'How High The Moon'. Though it was set up for music, the Countdown was not soundproofed and after only two or three weeks, the neighbours served the club with a noise injunction. As this was their only paying gig, the band even offered to play acoustically. The club had an upright piano for Rick, Syd and Bob Klose strummed acoustic guitars, Nick used wire brushes like a proper lounge act and Roger somehow managed to find an upright double bass.

Klose had been falling behind with his studies and both his father and his tutors blamed his failing grades on the band. When he failed his first year exams his father told him: 'No more music, you must study now' and that was the end of his career with the Pink Floyd. Though he played a few surreptitious gigs with them, he could no longer practice at college or play at college gigs. The band lost their most accomplished musician which essentially meant that they could no longer hope to remain an R&B band; they were not good enough players. The band's activities had also affected Roger's studies and he was held back a year. The staff thought he needed practical experience before going on to the next stage and arranged for him to work in an architectural practice. Nick, meanwhile, headed off to Guildford to do a year's work experience in the architectural offices of Frank Rutter, the father of his girlfriend Lindy, and appears to have enjoyed it. In his book he shows a lot of respect for Rutter, both as a person and as an architect. The practice was in Rutter's family house in Thursley, south of Guildford, which was large enough to house his staff and also accommodate his family and friends, including Nick. The large grounds enabled the staff to play croquet on the lawn during their lunch break.

The band were sometimes hired for parties out of town and at one such, the 21st birthday party of Libby January, Storm Thorgerson's girlfriend, in Cambridge, they found themselves sharing the bill with Joker's Wild which may have been the first time that Nick and Rick met the Joker's lead guitarist and vocalist, David Gilmour, unless they previously met when the London band members came up to visit; Nick is known to have enjoyed weekend visits to Roger's mother's house. Gradually, inexorably, the band was getting itself together.

*'Lucy Leave' and 'I'm A King Bee' have since appeared on various bootlegs but the other two fascinating-sounding originals remain unheard.
*Waters says 8 pm–1 am, Wright says 9 pm–2 am).

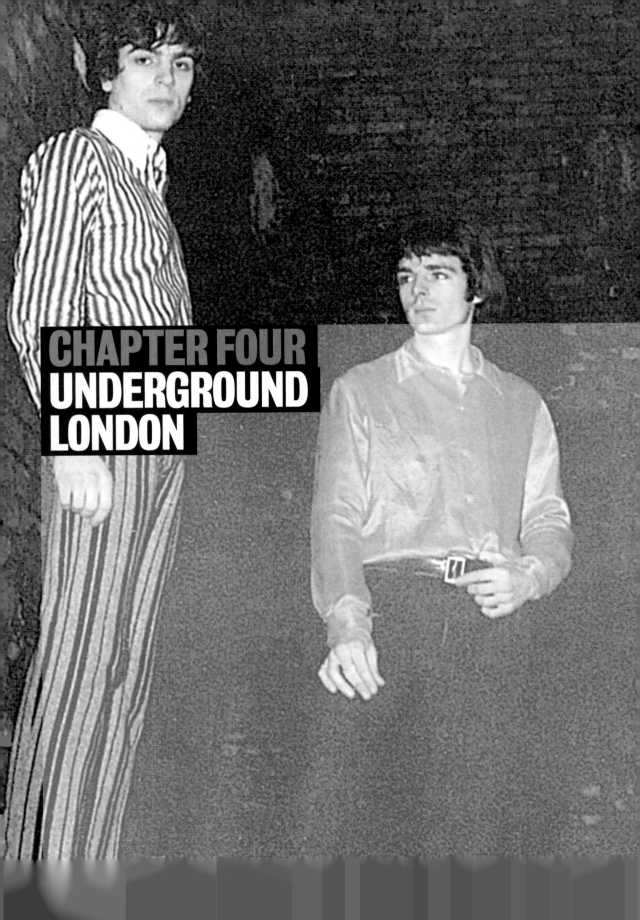

CHAPTER FOUR
UNDERGROUND LONDON

Right: Visually Syd
Barrett was the
most convincing
sartorial model
for psychedelia
in Pink Floyd.

CHAPTER FOUR
UNDERGROUND
LONDON

Many Pink Floyd gig chronologies list the group playing at the
Goings On Club, held once a week in a gambling club in Archer
Street, Soho, and organised by the poet Pete Brown who later went
on to co-write a number of hits for Cream with his friend Jack Bruce.
It was a short lived club; by the fifth week so many gamblers had
infiltrated themselves back in that the atmosphere was no longer
conducive to poetry and spontaneous happenings so it closed.
I think I attended them all, but I have no memory of seeing the
Pink Floyd play there (which is not to say they didn't).

Nigel Fountain's *Underground: The London Alternative Press
1966-1974* suggests that I saw the Pink Floyd play there as the Ab
Dabs [sic], but this is a mis-transcription of the original interview
tape, which was recorded by someone else, or a misunderstanding
on the author's part. I never did see them there, or as the Abdabs.
The club was more dedicated to poetry and performance art than
to music. My then wife, Sue, mixes the Goings On Club up with the
Spontaneous Underground Club in her description of it in Jonathon
Green's *Days In The Life*, which may be where the idea originates from. There were
a lot of performance art events at the time in London, for instance there was a
thoroughly disagreeable installation by Jeff Nuttall in Better Books at the time David
Gale worked there in late 1964 which involved a maze with 'air-locks' made from
phone books you had to push through and a tunnel filled with feathers that one
had to crawl through, among other things. John Lennon was not amused when he
emerged, covered in feathers.

SPONTANEOUS UNDERGROUND

The back room of Better Books had a low stage, rickety tables and chairs made from
different textures of wood, and a coffee/tea/soup machine. It was here, in the summer
of 1965, that Allen Ginsberg, Barbara Rubin, Dan Richter, Sue Miles, myself and
others first planned the idea of a poetry reading at the Royal Albert Hall. I was
managing the shop and had already put on a reading by Ginsberg which was so
overcrowded that people fainted. Now both Gregory Corso and Lawrence Ferlinghetti
were coming to town and we wanted a venue that would hold the audience that the
three premier Beat poets would attract. This reading is generally considered to be the
genesis of the London underground and counter-cultural scene, spawning, among
other things, the *International Times* underground newspaper (*IT*) and the London
Free School. But it was not just Londoners who were inspired by it.

On her return to New York, Allen Ginsberg's off-and-on girlfriend, Barbara Rubin,
the one who had actually booked the Albert Hall, made plans for a follow-up event
the next year to feature the Fugs, the Chambers Brothers and Timothy Leary, films
by Warhol, as well as Allen Ginsberg and a number of other New York poets. Closely

involved with Barbara's plans was Bernard Stollman, the owner of ESP-Disk, the experimental jazz label that released the Fugs as well as Albert Ayler, the New York Art Quartet and many even more 'difficult' artists. He was interested in finding new artists in London and had already made plans to release a recording by William Burroughs – *Call Me Burroughs* – that Barbara brought back from Better Books. (It was privately pressed in Paris and I was the UK distributor.)

Hoping to locate more unusual recordings along this line, Bernard encouraged his younger brother Steve, a film-maker and an active participant in the downtown New York art scene, to go to London to look for new acts. He arrived around the Christmas of 1965, and immediately met up with all the members of the inchoate underground who had been involved with the Albert Hall reading. There were so many people doing things, and the London scene was so spread out compared to New York, that Steve decided to start a club and have them come to him. He figured that if you provided the space for people to get together and perform, then things would happen spontaneously.

There had already been evidence of this with the Goings On Club and other happenings and performance events. Steve rented the Marquee Club, at 90 Wardour Street, on a Sunday afternoon and charged six shillings and sixpence admission to pay the rental. He made no profit from it. Though the Pink Floyd did not play at the first Spontaneous Underground, it is worth describing it in detail as it gives a good idea of the London scene that they were about to launch themselves into and introduces some of the characters who were to play an integral part in their story.

There were no ads for the events which were by invitation only, in these days before most people had telephones the usual method of communication was the mimeographed flyer. It was very important to have a good mailing list. Several lists were combined and invitations were sent out to key people consisting of an envelope filled with William Burroughs style cut-ups – each unique. There were slivers from Alexander Trocchi's *Sigma Portfolio*, slices of discarded pages from *Long Hair* magazine and a couple of inches cut from a Marvel comic.

For the first event there was a mimeo statement which read:

> **SPONTANEOUS UNDERGROUND at the Marquee this Sunday January 30th organised by Steve Stollman of ESP Disk with the aid of everybody. Among those taking part will be Donovan/Mose Allison/Graham Bond/Pop/Mime/Kinetic Sculpture/Discotheque/Boutique. THIS TRIP begins at 4.30 and goes on. Liquor licence applied for. Costume, masque, ethnic, space, Edwardian, Victorian and hipness generally...face and body makeup—certainly. This is a spontaneous party, any profit to be held in trust by Louis Diamond, Solicitor, that such spontaneities may continue. Invitation only, donation at door 6/6.**

The *Sunday Times* previewed the event under the heading 'Revolutionary Party Organiser':

"An absolutely new kind of rave," claims John Hopkins, who helped to make up the star-spangled invitation list for a massive *soirée*, to be held this evening at the Marquee Club, London... . The organiser, 23-year-old Steve Stollman, until recently, made documentary films in America. Now he wants to make documentary "happenings" in England. The invited *are* the entertainment... Who will be there? Poets, painters, pop singers, hoods, Americans, homosexuals ("because they make up 10 per cent of the population"), 20 clowns, jazz musicians, "one murderer", sculptors, politicians and some girls who defy description are among those invited. For Stollman their identity is irrelevant because this is underground culture which offers everyone the opportunity to do or say anything without conforming to the restrictions of earthmen..."

It was a great success; many of the people who had been involved with the Goings On club came along. There was nothing to do on Sundays in London in those days, in fact the whole event was probably illegal; these were the days when park attendants still chained up the swings in children's playgrounds on the Sabbath in some parts of the country. It was not until 1969 that most parts of the 18th century Sunday Observance laws were relaxed.

True to the spirit of the club people arrived at the Marquee in fancy dress, proto-hippie gear and the sort of combination bowler hat and ex-war department look favoured by trad bands on the Aldermaston CND route. Just across Oxford Street from

Wardour Street was the garment district, then much bigger because there were still a lot of sweat shops in the area. The bins outside these light industrial buildings were filled with fabric offcuts, and often several yards of material would still be left on a spool. Great bundles of cardboard tubes, originally wrapped with cloth, stood stacked in doorways. Enterprising young women dragged armloads of this material down to the Marquee where others had come equipped with scissors and paste, crepe paper and everything needed for a fancy dress production line. Not everyone needed them; Donovan arrived later in the day wearing thick black kohl and henna eye make-up: each eye drawn with an Egyptian Eye of Horus. He sat cross-legged on the stage and sang with six sitar players and a conga drummer but the next day he had no memory of ever being there.

Johnny Byrne* and the poet Spike Hawkins did an anarchic double-act as the Poison Bellows and arrived pushing a wind-up gramophone in an old pram wearing long overcoats and mufflers and trailing yards and yards of fabric they had found in the street and looking a lot like Peter Cook and Dudley Moore. They performed inept anti-conjuring tricks using Pete Brown's father's antique collapsible silk top hat; the magically produced eggs were inevitably broken so that Johnny's collar was covered with egg shells. It was the type of British slapstick humour typified by the Alberts that finds something inherently funny about a tuba. The Bonzo Dog Doo-Dah Band had it, and to a certain extent the Scaffold. It had its immediate genesis in *The Goon Show* and reached its peak with *Monty Python's Flying Circus* but the Poison Bellows had a harder edge. Johnny told Jonathon Green: 'One of the things that happens in any movement is that people accept anything and we simply wanted to shock them out of that.' It didn't last long because part of the act involved an enormously heavy pianola that the duo had no means to transport.

Before Donovan arrived, Graham Bond did his mystical pirate act but Mose Allison did not show. It didn't matter – the audience was the real entertainment. Being Sunday no alcohol was allowed but it was not needed, as Steve said: 'People will be high enough on entertainment alone' and, of course, many were high when they got there.

The 'Spontaneous Underground' immediately became the village pump of the underground. It had something of the atmosphere of the Albert Hall reading except the Marquee gathering became a regular event. The next invite was a promotional insert for ESP Records with a faint two colour Roneoed message overprinted and bleeding off the page on both sides of the card – barely decipherable and lacking a date, rather like rave invites in the Nineties, it read:

> **In memoriam. King Charles. Marquis de Sade. Superman. Supergirl. Ulysses. Charlie Chaplin. All tripping lightly looning phoenician moon mad sailors – in characteri as IN characters – characterised in costume at the Marquee this Sunday at 5 o clock...**

The information given was the literary equivalent of a psychedelic poster, it suggested an attitude, a mood, a state of mind, an approach. As the activities continued there were many memorable events: the time a classical pianist calmly played her way through the Bach Preludes and Fugues surrounded by Ginger Johnson and his African Drummers who pounded out cross rhythms all around her, highlighting the good bits with trumpet reveilles and bringing out something called 'the Big Log' – a hollowed out tree trunk – for the grand finale.

The lights remained on during performances; after all there was not supposed to be a division between audience and performers though by end of this particular set the stage was enveloped in a thick cloud of pot smoke like the dry ice which bands used later, only more fun. The lack of division between stage and audience was emphasized on one occasion by a young woman who had her long red Rapunzel hair trimmed by a friend on stage where the lighting was better while musicians honked and hooted all around her.

Many of the pick-up bands involved members of the early, ever-changing personnel of the Soft Machine: Robert Wyatt on drums; Daevid Allen singing or sometimes reading his poems; the illustrator Mal Dean whose Jerry Cornelius strip and cartoons later enlivened *International Times*, on trumpet and lavatory plunger; Rab Spall on amplified violin, John Surman on soprano saxophone. There were two conga drummers who appeared regularly, also several spoons players – buskers still used this instrument while entertaining cinema queues. Then there were the extra-musical events. It was at one of the Spontaneous Underground events that Gerry Fitzgerald

*Byrne later co-wrote the book *Groupie* with Jenny Fabian about her exciting friendships with rock 'n' roll musicians including Syd Barrett.

MIDDLE
EARTH
PINK FLOYD
1967

first presented one of his enormous jellies. A large heap of pink jelly became a regular feature of early London underground events and someone inevitably stripped off and rolled in it.

Though people always referred to it as Spontaneous Underground, the announcements for the Sunday afternoon events at the Marquee only ever used that name once. Steve called it The Trip, as in his announcement for the March 13th event. This was the first time the Pink Floyd Sound played there, though by this stage in the club's history no bands were advertised:

TRIP bring furniture toy prop paper rug paint balloon jumble costume mask robot candle incense ladder wheel light self all others march 13th 5pm

The notion of there being no division between performers and audience was particularly suited to AMM, for whom all sounds constituted part of the piece being performed, whether they originated in the group or the audience. There was no melody, no rhythm and no score. Cornelius Cardew – who played piano, cello and transistor radio – though he rarely, if ever, touched the notes of the piano, preferring to pluck the strings or tap on the frame – wrote 'An AMM performance has no beginning or ending. Sounds outside the performance are distinguished from it only by individual sensibility.'

Cardew studied with Stockhausen, had worked with John Cage and David Tudor in Europe and had prepared a guitar version of Cage's *Fontana Mix*. The other members were Lou Gare on tenor saxophone and violin, Eddie Provost on drums, xylophone and various percussion, Lawrence Sheaff on cello, accordion, clarinet and transistor radio and Keith Rowe on electric guitar and transistor radio. This was free-form music at its cutting edge and to reinforce the sense of serious scientific investigation AMM played in white lab coats. The idea that all sound could have a musical value was absorbed by the Pink Floyd who later took up the idea and spent hours using non-conventional musical sources to try and make an album. Some of the sounds AMM made were impossible to identify. Watching from the side of the stage Syd Barrett was intrigued to see that Keith Rowe achieved some of his special effects on electric guitar by rolling steel ball bearings up and down the strings to produce peculiar sounds.

Syd borrowed this procedure and later used it himself on stage. Keith Rowe had an enormous influence on Syd's playing, as can be seen in Peter Whitehead's *Pink Floyd London 1966/1967* film where Syd spends most of his time on the studio recordings of 'Interstellar Overdrive', and an improvised jam called 'Nick's Boogie,' using his guitar in the slide position – 'table top position' as Rowe called it – producing effects rather than any recognisable melodies or improvisation on the tunes.

Rowe came from a fine art background and had always been very attracted to the idea of the 'found object' and Marcel Duchamp's assertion that "Whatever the artists chooses to be art is art." At the beginning of the Sixties Rowe had been a member of Mike Westbrook's band until his resolution never to tune the guitar again made his departure from the group inevitable. Inspired by John Cage's 'prepared piano' he developed his own 'prepared guitar' placing objects on or between the strings to alter the guitar's timbre and using other extended techniques to push his music into the realm of complete abstraction.

The Pink Floyd Sound were elated to be playing the Marquee, thinking that this might be the break they needed to get onto the London club circuit, so it was somewhat disconcerting for them to find that they were playing at what appeared to be a private event. There was little connection between the Spontaneous Underground crowd and the normal Marquee audiences though the wife of the club owner Harold Pendleton, was there to keep an eye on things and the Floyd's reception was duly noted. Whereas the house lights were usually kept on for the Sunday events, in this instance they were lowered, as were the stage lights, in order for a film and light show to play over the group.

Two days before, still using the name Tea Set, they had played the Rag Ball at Essex University in Colchester – where they shared the bill with the Swinging Blue Jeans – and someone had projected a film accompanied by oil-based slides onto the stage backdrop as they played. Roger Waters told Michael Wale: "We'd already become interested in mix-media, as it were, and some bright spark down there had had done a film with a paraplegic in London, given this paraplegic a film camera and wheeled him round London, filming his view. Now they showed it up on screen as we played." The band were intrigued by the possibilities of combining a light-show with their music

'The LFS offers you free education through lectures and discussion groups in subjects essential to our daily life and work.'

John Hopkins

The film of London shot at a low angle view was certainly shown at the Spontaneous Underground so it was probably screened at this event, but not even the most dedicated Pink Floyd researchers seem to know who projected it and provided the light-show. Steve Stollman and Hoppy were both delighted with the group's performance, which featured extended free-form improvisation on old R&B classics, and invited them back. The band themselves were pleased to find such a sympathetic audience and returned on a number of occasions. Nick Mason told *Mojo*: "There were elements of the underground that we did tune into. The main one was mixed media. We may not have been into acid but we certainly understood the idea of a Happening. We supplied the music while people did creative dance, painted their faces or bathed in the giant jelly. If it had been 30 years earlier Rick would have come up out of the floor in front of the cinema screen playing the organ."

The Pink Floyd Sound became the public face of the London underground scene, even though, with the exception of Syd, they were actually somewhat removed from it. Roger Waters: "The whole mixed media thing started happening in 1966. We had a Sunday afternoon at the Marquee with film going and us banging and crashing away. John Hopkins and his merry men were there. By this time there were one or two names creeping over from the West Coast like Moby Grape, Jefferson Airplane, the Grateful Dead. Nobody had heard them.'

Most of the San Francisco bands did not release any albums in Britain until the summer of 1967, long after the Pink Floyd, the Soft Machine and the other British 'psychedelic' bands had developed their own styles so there was never a question of them being influenced by the American groups. In fact, when they did finally get to hear them they were disappointed to find that most of them were just blues bands; quite good but not breaking any new ground at all. It is unclear how many times the Pink Floyd played the Spontaneous Underground. Published gig lists show them as the house band, but the event was not a regular one: John Hopkins can only remember attending one and I can only remember three. In all probability there were less than half a dozen and it is certain that the Pink Floyd did not play them all.

LONDON FREE SCHOOL

Five days before the Pink Floyd played at the Spontaneous Underground, a group of people, many of whom were associated with the club, embarked on another underground enterprise. The London Free School was launched at a public meeting at St Peter's Church Hall, Notting Hill, on Tuesday, March 8, 1966. The red and black flyer printed by John Hopkins read, "The LFS offers you free education through lectures and discussion groups in subjects essential to our daily life and work." It promised that "The London Free School is not political, not racial, not intellectual, not religion, not a club. It is open to all."

It was basically an alternative community centre, offering 24-hour free legal advice and assistance to the local largely West Indian population, running a pre-school nursery, lessons on English and other similar services. It was designed to "promote co-operation and understanding between people of various races and creeds through education and through working together." Notting Hill was not the millionaires' playground it is now; in the mid Sixties it was a run down area of decaying Regency houses shoddily converted into cheap flats, with a large West Indian population mercilessly exploited by slum landlords like Peter Rachman.

The LFS, aside from being the launch pad for the Pink Floyd, is best known as the organisation that founded the Notting Hill Carnival. There had been a Notting Hill Fayre and Pageant which stopped around the turn of the century, but following in the wake of the 1958 Notting Hill race riots the tradition was revived by Claudia Jones, a Trinidadian member of the Communist Party who arrived in London in 1955 who proposed that a Caribbean carnival was the best response to the racists. She organised a cabaret programme at St. Pancras Town Hall, complete with steel bands and a carnival queen beauty contest, on January 30, 1959 following a small procession in Powis Square, Notting Hill. The event was a great success and continued for seven years at various venues, including Porchester Hall and Seymour Hall where, in 1962, calypso king Mighty Sparrow played. The carnival ceased when Claudia Jones died of chronic heart disease in 1964.

It began in its present form, as a summer festival, two years later when Rhaunie Laslett, a social worker of Native American and Russian descent, known locally as Miss Las, became the first president of the London Free School. Though she must have known of Claudia Jones's West Indian carnival – and surely attended it – she famously claimed that the idea came to her in a dream: she saw a multitude of people dressed in colourful costumes, a street procession where black and white people got to know and understand each other's customs and created an atmosphere of warmth and happiness throughout Notting Hill. Paddington council offered a large grant towards the resurrection of the Notting Hill Carnival, but only if the LFS got rid of Michael de Freitas.

Michael had been a pimp and an enforcer for Peter Rachman – it was Michael who would go in with German Shepherds to evict recalcitrant tenants (who were for the most part West Indians). Michael had a criminal reputation and liked to boast that he had once killed a man with a machete. Some years later he was convicted of doing just this by a court in Trinidad and sentenced to death by hanging but that was in the future. In 1966 he was experiencing a number of major changes in life, one of which was his conversion to the Muslim faith, as preached by Elijah Muhammad and his Black Muslim organisation in the States. Michael changed his name, first to Michael X, then to Michael Abdul Malik in keeping with his new religion.

Michael contributed a lot to the Free School, setting up an adventure playground for the local kids on Acklam Road and – his most impressive contribution as far as drawing attention to the Free School – persuading Muhammad Ali, then the heavyweight champion of the World in the run up to his second Henry Cooper fight, to visit Rhaunie Laslett's neighbourhood law centre and childrens' playgroup at 34 Tavistock Crescent. Ali arrived on May 15, 1966, wearing a Beatles-style suit, sat on the floor and chatted with the 50 youngsters gathered there, signed autographs and talked with the excited crowd that had gathered outside, blocking the street. 'Are you happy?' someone shouted. 'I'm happy *here*!' he said.

Hoppy and Rhaunie Laslett refused to be blackmailed by Paddington council and insisted that Michael stay involved as one of the ways to connect with the West Indian community and in July 1966 the first Notting Hill Carnival happened anyway, without the council's help. Many of the same group of activists, artists and musicians that were to play a role in the development of the London underground scene: John Hopkins, Graham Keen, Peter Jenner and Dave Tomlin, were organisers. Artists involved with the first Carnival included Ginger Johnson and the Afro Cuban Band, the New Orleans Marching Band, Agnes O'Connell's London Irish Girl Pipers and Nell Gwynne riding in a horse drawn orange cart, but the real energy in the parade came from a Caribbean steel band.

Russell Henderson, Sterling Betancourt, Vernon 'Fellows' Williams, and Ralph Cherry led a parade of floats with children in fancy dress. Apparently as they passed by, people rushed to the street to join them, leaving their meals burning on the stoves or dancing with their hair still wet with shampoo, the band was so good; there was a real carnival atmosphere and about 1,000 West Indians and 1,500 white people filled the streets. There were poetry readings and competition darts matches and all manner of events. The Fair continued for a whole week and there were remarkably few arrests, despite a heavy police presence. From this humble beginning, the Notting Hill Carnival has now grown to become the largest street carnival in Europe, attracting more than a million people to the streets of Notting Hill every August Bank Holiday weekend.

There was a good cross-section of people at the LFS; one of them, for instance, was director John Huston's daughter, the actress Anjelica who was then attending nearby Holland Park Comprehensive when she wasn't hanging out in the LFS's psychedelic basement headquarters at 26 Powis Terrace. She remembers playing "a good deal of hooky in the basement of a fish and chip shop in Powis Terrace called the London Free School. We used to spend many a happy afternoon with a bunch of bright hippies doing what I care not to remember... To come into one's age in London... I remember hearing Bob Dylan for the first time and Otis Redding for the first time and going to see Ike and Tina Turner at the Revolution. Not to mention the Beatles, the Rolling Stones, the Roundhouse, Eel Pie Island. It was something that was unprecedented and I think it threw everyone into a state but it was awfully good fun if you were on the cusp of it."

'a good deal of hooky in the basement of a fish and chip shop in Powis Terrace called the London Free School. We used to spend many a happy afternoon with a bunch of bright hippies doing what I care not to remember...'

Anjelica

CHAPTER FIVE
LONDON FREE SCHOOL & INTERNATIONAL TIMES

Right: The Floyd
celebrate Syd's
22nd birthday
in a photo shoot
for Fabulous
208 magazine,
January 1968.

CHAPTER FIVE
LONDON FREE SCHOOL & INTERNATIONAL TIMES

At the Spontaneous Underground held on 13 June 1966, the Pink Floyd met their future manager Peter Jenner, an assistant sociology lecturer at the London School of Economics and one of the people involved with starting the London Free School. Peter was a great follower of experimental music and was one of the founders of DNA Productions, set up to record avant garde jazz and so-called modern classical music by John Hopkins, Felix de Mendelsohn and two jazz critics Ron Atkins and Alan Beckett. Their first production had been *AMMMUSIC* by AMM released by Hoppy's friend, the American tour promoter and producer Joe Boyd, who now worked for Jac Holzman at Elektra Records. Next they recorded an album with American Steve Lacy, but it was not released, possibly because when they analysed the deal with Elektra – the standard 2% production royalty – they realised that they would have to sell tens of thousands of records in order to make any money after recording costs. The only way to make money as producers was to have a hit record and that meant rock 'n' roll. Peter began searching for a band to produce, he wanted something challenging but more commercial than the music he had already recorded.

Earlier that summer, Kate Heliczer returned to Britain having spent some time living in New York as part of Andy Warhol's downtown Factory scene. She knew Warhol's assistant Gerard Malanga and Lou Reed and brought with her tapes of the Velvet Underground playing at Warhol's Exploding Plastic Inevitable. Peter was very impressed with the tapes, but by the time he got through to John Cale on the phone, Warhol had decided to go into record production himself and had already recorded the Velvets. It was a Sunday in June and Jenner was fed up with marking exams so he decided to call it a day and wander down to the Marquee to see what was going on at the Spontaneous Underground.

"I arrived around 10:30," he recalled, "and there on stage was this strange band who were playing a mixture of R&B and electronic noises. In between the routine stuff like 'Louie Louie' and 'Road Runner' they were playing these very weird breaks. It was all very bizarre and just what I was looking for – a far out, electronic, freaky pop group... and there, across their bass amp was their name: 'The Pink Floyd Sound.'"

Jenner was puzzled by the sounds the group were making; he couldn't figure out if they were coming from the organ or the guitar. Syd was using a Binson Echorec, an echo unit, probably the B2 introduced in 1962, and most celebrated by being used by Hank Marvin of the Shadows.* It had twelve settings and two foot pedal sockets, giving him an enormous range of possibilities of sound, particularly when he used his zippo lighter as a plectrum.

Rick Wright: "That was a very special time. Those early days were purely experimental for us and a time of learning and finding out exactly what we were trying

*The claim that Syd was the first
guitarist to use this is nonsense.
Binson had been making them since
the late Fifties.

INTERNATIONAL TIMES FIRST
ALL-NIGHT RAVE

POP OP COSTUME MASQUE DRAG BALL ET AL

STRIP TRIP/HAPPENINGS/MOVIES
SOFT MACHINE/PINK FLOYD STEEL BAND

SUR PRIZE FOR SHORTEST-BAREST

ROUND HOUSE (OPP CHALK FARM TUBE)
SAT 15 OCTOBER 11 PM ONWARDS
5 SHILLINGS IN ADVANCE 10 SHILLINGS DOOR

BRING YOUR OWN POISON

Above: Tickets for the launch party for International Times at the Roundhouse.

to do. Each night was a complete buzz because we did totally new things and none of us knew how the others would react to it. It was the formation of the Pink Floyd."

Jenner realised that he could not manage a band by himself and discussed it with his old school friend Andrew King, an educational cyberneticist, who had recently left his job at the British Airways training and education department and was at a loose end. King agreed to become his partner and together they visited Mike Leonard's house in Stanhope Gardens and offered to manage them. Roger Waters described their meeting: "As far as I remember he must have come to a gig, maybe it was one of those funny things at the Marquee. But he and Andrew King approached us and said, 'You lads could be bigger than the Beatles!' and we sort of looked at him and replied in a dubious tone 'Yes, well we'll see you when we get back from our hols,' because we were all shooting off for some sun on the Continent."

Roger was going to Greece with a group of friends including Rick Wright and it was there he took acid for the first and only time. He didn't have a bad time, but found the experience so powerful that he felt no need to repeat it. In those days it was common to take massive doses, usually in liquid form where there was no accurate way of measuring the amount. He told John Harris: "I took it and thought I was coming out the other end, and went to the window in the room where I was – and I stood on the spot for another three hours. Just *frozen*." This was probably also the time when Rick Wright first took it.

Nick Mason was already away, having gone to New York where his girlfriend Lindy was training with the Martha Graham Dance Company. He saw the Fugs play the Players Theatre on Bleeker Street and both Mose Allison and Thelonius Monk at the Village Vanguard, then he and Lindy bought two of the famous $99 unlimited travel Greyhound tickets and set out to explore America, visiting San Francisco and even going down to Mexico City and spending time in Acapulco where hotel rooms were only a dollar a night. After three months they returned to New York. Nick had not thought much about the Pink Floyd while he was away, in fact when he left the band had been on the point of breaking up; gigs were hard to come by, they had no proper equipment, and rehearsals were interfering with their studies. He thought that on his return to London he would be once more immersed in his architectural studies.

Then, in New York, he bought a copy of the local underground newspaper, the *East Village Other*, or *EVO* as it was known, with a report on the London underground scene that mentioned the Pink Floyd Sound as the most interesting of the new bands. In *Inside Out, A Personal History of Pink Floyd*, he wrote: 'Finding this name check so far from home really gave me a new perception of the band. Displaying a touchingly naïve trust in the fact that you can believe everything you read in the newspapers, it made me realise that the band had the potential to be more than simply a vehicle for our own amusement.'

I was the London correspondent for *EVO* and I am proud to say that I was the author of this piece which was, oddly enough, the first press coverage the Pink Floyd ever had outside the Poly student paper. It is even nicer to feel that it may have helped encourage the band to stick it out though this was much more down to the efforts of Peter Jenner and Andrew King. Seeing that they were serious about managing them, and providing them with new, much needed equipment, the band agreed to let them manage them, though Roger and Nick secretly thought that Jenner and King were drug dealers.

Though Syd was already smoking pot and writing songs, it was not until 1966, when he was 20, that he took his first trip.[*] Syd, along with Storm Thorgeson, Nigel Gordon and Ian 'Imo' Moore, was visiting his friend Bob Gale in his garden in Cambridge. Thorgeson and Imo had laid out hundreds of sugar cubes in rows and were treating each one with two drops of liquid LSD from a glass bottle. The acid was very concentrated and as they licked the sugar granules from their fingers they became hopelessly confused, giving some cubes a double dose and others none at all. Imo has often told the well known story of how Syd found three objects: an orange, a plum and a matchbox and sat and stared at them for twelve hours. The plum became the planet Venus and the orange was Jupiter. Syd travelled between them in outer space. His trip came to an abrupt end when Imo, feeling hungry, ate Venus in one bite. "You should have seen Syd's face. He was in total shock for a few seconds, then he just grinned."

Nigel Gordon: "We were all seeking higher elevation and wanted everyone to experience this incredible drug. Syd was very self-obsessed and uptight in many ways so we thought it was a good idea. In retrospect I don't think he was equipped to deal

[*] Syd and his circle had already experimented with magic mushrooms – an experience documented on an 8-mm colour film shot by Nigel Gordon in the Gog Magog hills outside Cambridge. The footage has been widely bootlegged on video and DVD under the erroneous title *Syd's First Trip*.

with the experience because he was unstable to begin with. Syd was a very simple person who was having very profound experiences that he found it hard to deal with."

Syd and his new co-manager Jenner spent the summer of 1966 listening to Love's eponymous debut album and *Fifth Dimension* by the Byrds. This gave rise to one of the Pink Floyd's most emblematic numbers, 'Interstellar Overdrive.' Jenner had tried to hum Arthur Lee's guitar hook from Love's version of Burt Bacharach's 'My Little Red Book' to Syd, but what Syd played back sounded quite different and he used the chord changes to write 'Interstellar Overdrive.' Jenner and Barrett also took a lot of acid together and became very close.

Though the Pink Floyd became the symbol of psychedelic music in Britain, the other members of the group were more reserved, and had little to do with drugs. In fact Nick Mason didn't even regard Syd as part of the underground scene: "I don't think Syd was a man of the times. He didn't slot in with the intellectual likes of John Hopkins and Joe Boyd, Miles, Pete Jenner, the London Free School people. Probably being middle class we could talk our way through, make ourselves sound as though we were part of it.... But Syd was a great figurehead. He was part of acid culture."

This was one of the biggest differences between the British and American West Coast scenes: in San Francisco bands like the Grateful Dead and the Jefferson Airplane lived communally in Haight-Ashbury and contributed to the psychedelic community. In Britain, though many individual band members were sympathetic to what was happening on the underground such as Pete Townshend, none of the major bands were actually part of the community (except Hawkwind, later). There were very few benefits or free concerts and, perhaps more importantly, no money funding the community from that source. The Pink Floyd, with the exception of Syd, had barely an inkling of the community who had embraced and supported them. Roger: "You'd hear about revolution, but it was never terribly specific. I don't know... I read *International Times* a few times. But, you know, what was the Notting Hill Free School actually all about? What was it meant to do?"

In order to find out, he would have had to get involved and maybe even contribute something himself, but the band were too concerned with becoming pop stars for that. The underground was a convenient stepping stone, to be used and discarded. People who compare the Floyd's role in the London scene with that of the Dead or Jefferson Airplane in San Francisco are sadly deluded; in reality the Floyd were neither psychedelic nor underground; as they were very quick to point out once they signed with a major record company.

BLACKHILL PRODUCTIONS

At this time, the Pink Floyd was still, as it were, a straight band. Nick Mason: "At that time we were aiming to be a hit parade band. I mean – we wanted a hit single. The idea of making an album hadn't even... well, I'm speaking personally, 'cause I can't speak for the others, but I suspect that we hadn't really considered the sort of move onto an album. We were only interested in making a single initially, and a hit single. We were interested in the business of being in rock'n'roll, and being a pop group: SUCCESSFUL – MONEY – CARS, that sort of thing. Good living. I mean, that's... umm, that's the reason most people get involved in rock music, because they want that sort of success. If you don't, you get involved in something else."

Despite their pop aspirations, a company was set up much more in the spirit of the time called Blackhill Productions, named after a cottage that Andrew King had bought in the Brecon Beacons of Wales with a small inheritance. The shareholding was split six ways, giving each of them, managers and band, a one sixth share in the company. This was an extraordinary arrangement when you consider that a typical deal at the time was like Brian Epstein's with the Beatles: he took 25% off the top before any of the massive expenses – including his own – were paid, and the Beatles divided what was left between the four of them, making him far wealthier than any of them.

King spent the remainder of his legacy on equipment and the band began rehearsing. The equipment was almost immediately stolen and new amps had to be bought on hire purchase. In the interim, Peter Asher, of the pop duo Peter and Gordon, who was a partner in the Indica Gallery and Bookshop and possibly knew Peter Jenner and Andrew King from Westminster school, lent them his backing band's equipment.

Unfortunately neither King nor Jenner knew anything about booking gigs but just then, two requirements happened to coincide fortuitously. One was the Pink Floyd Sound's need to perform and the other was that the London Free School needed to

The International Times No 8 Feb 13-26 1967/1s
ginsberg • townshend (who) • snyder • mandrake root

Above: London Free School flyer and an early issue of IT.

'Those were halcyon days. He'd sit around with copious amounts of hash and grass and write these incredible songs. There's no doubt they were crafted very carefully and deliberately.'

Peter Jenner

raise money. It was John ('Hoppy') Hopkins who thought of the idea of a benefit concert, but as both Peter and Andrew were vicars' sons, it seems likely that it was one of them who came up with the idea of holding it in a church hall; they must have had plenty of experience of such events in their childhood.

All Saints Hall, on Powis Square (though advertised as being on Powis Gardens) was a traditional church hall – high ceiling, wooden floor, multi-purpose stage at the far end – and possibly not what the Floyd were expecting as a venue. However all went well. In fact, if UFO was the Pink Floyd's Cavern Club, then All Saints Hall was their Star Club, albeit a very truncated version in terms of time, in both cases.

The evenings were called 'Sound Light Workshops' and the Pink Floyd took this seriously. I described one of their sets – using the breathless, underground style of the time – as taking "musical innovation further out than it had ever been before, walking out on incredibly dangerous limbs and dancing along crumbling precipices, saved sometimes only by the confidence beamed at them from the audience sitting a matter of inches away at their feet. Ultimately, having explored to their satisfaction, Nick would begin the drum roll that led to the final run through of the theme [to 'Interstellar Overdrive'] and everyone could breathe again.'

The first event, on September 30, 1966, was not very well-attended, in fact there were so few people that at one point Syd entertained the audience with the soliloqy from *Hamlet*, but word soon got around. Notting Hill was then the centre of London's underground, counter-cultural hippie scene, and the London Free School was central to what was happening. Two weeks later the Floyd played All Saints Hall again and the place was more or less full. Hoppy's mimeographed flyer read:

ANNOUNCING; POP DANCE FEATURING LONDON'S FARTHEST-OUT GROUP THE PINK FLOYD IN INTERSTELLAR OVERDRIVE STONED ALONE ASTRONOMY DOMINI (an astral chant) & other numbers from their space-age book also: LIGHT PROJECTION SLIDES LIQUID MOVIES THE TIME: 8-11 PM THE DAY: FRIDAY 14 OCTOBER THE PLACE: ALL SAINT'S HALL, POWIS GARDENS, W11 THE REASON: GOOD TIMES ANOTHER LONDON FREE SCHOOL PRODUCTION.

The last of the Pink Floyd Sound Light Workshops at the London Free School, held on November 29, was reviewed for *International Times* by the Soft Machine's original Californian lead guitarist, Larry Nolan: "Since I last saw the Pink Floyd they've got hold of bigger amplifiers, new light gear and a rave from Paul McCartney... Their work is largely improvisation, and lead guitarist Syd Barrett shoulders most of the burden of providing continuity and attack in the improvised parts. He was providing a huge range of sounds with the new equipment, from throttled shrieks to mellow feedback roars. Visually the show was less adventurous. Three projectors bathed the group, the walls and sometimes the audience in vivid colour. But the colour was fairly static, and there was no searching for the brain alpha rhythms, by chopping the focus of the images. The equipment that the group is using now is infant electronics; lets see what they will do with the grownup electronics that a colour television industry will make available.'*

Each LFS concert featured bigger and better lights. The first time they played there, an American couple, Joel and Toni Brown, who had arrived in London from the League for Spiritual Dioscovery, Timothy Leary's psychedelic centre in Millbrook, New York, showed up with a slide projector and projected strange images onto the band in time with the music. It was rudimentary but both the band and their management reacted enthusiastically. It was the obvious complement to their long improvisations and, as news was already filtering in about bands using light shows in San Francisco, it seemed to be the next big thing. Peter Jenner and his new wife Sumi immediately set to work to build their own lighting rig for the band. It consisted of a row of ordinary spotlights mounted on a board with sheets of different coloured Perspex in front of them, each one operated by an ordinary household on-off switch. They were low powered but threw a huge shadow behind each member of the band which was very effective. Then Joey Gannon got involved. He was only 17 at the time but he knew people at the Hornsey College of Art Light/Sound workshop founded by Mike Leonard, and introduced a projector to the set-up.

Syd was now living at 2 Earlham Street with Peter Wynne-Willson who worked at the New Theatre in the West End and had easy access to discarded theatrical lighting

*Colour television was introduced to Britain via BBC-2 in the summer of 1967.

equipment which he renovated for the band. Peter and his girlfriend, Susie Gawler-Wright, became the Pink Floyd light-operators alongside Joey Gannon. Joey brought in some theatrical spotlights that he operated using a small keyboard built by Wynne-Willson. He also obtained a 500 watt and a 1000 watt projector. Wynne-Willson developed a way of painting blank slides with brightly coloured inks which became the liquid slides most associated with the London underground scene: he would heat the ink with a small blow torch and cool it with a hair dryer causing the ink to bubble and move. The team experimented with different chemicals and colours and each gig revealed new images and effects as they developed their techniques.

The flat at 2 Earlham Street, was just off Cambridge Circus on the edge of Soho in a row of low run-down old buildings (now demolished) dating back to before Shaftesbury Avenue was built. It was easily identifiable by its purple door. The street was lined with barrows selling used books, an adjunct to the bookshops on Charing Cross Road around the corner. Bargains were still to be found on Earlham Street and it was thronged with book runners, all looking for W.H. Auden's first book *Poems*, a copy of which had been found there in 1965 at the cost of one shilling and sold later that day to another dealer for a thousand pounds.

The flower and vegetable markets were still in Covent Garden at the time so it was possible to eat very cheaply on cast-offs or from the stalls in the market. The building was rented by Peter Wynne-Willson and Susie Gawler-Wright who, in the usual Sixties underground style, shared it with a group of ever changing roommates. Susie, with her long straight hair, and slender figure looked the archetypal 'hippie chick': "Wow" was her favourite word, said with an air of amused astonishment. She became known as the 'psychedelic debutante' as she apparently came from an aristocratic background. She famously featured on the front cover of *International Times* issue 11, naked except for psychedelic body paint.* Peter Wynne-Willson was also from an elevated background: his uncle was the Bishop of Bath and Wells and lived in a palace surrounded by a moat with swans.

Susie was a follower of Radha Soami Satsang, also known as Sant Mat, an Indian religious cult. This was a method of 'God-realisation' consisting of three parts: *simran*, or the repetition of the Lord's holy names. The second is *dhyan*, or contemplation on the immortal form of the Master. This keeps the student's attention fixed at the centre. The third is *bhajan*, or listening to the Anahad Shabd or celestial music that is constantly reverberating within us. This was perhaps what appealed to Syd Barrett; apparently, assisted by this divine melody, the soul ascends to higher regions to finally reach the feet of the Lord. Significantly Sant Mat took no money from its followers, unlike some of the Eastern organisations that grew in popularity with the hippies. Though Susie, Nigel Gordon and other Cambridge friends were initiated and given a secret mantra, Syd, inexplicably, was refused. The Maharaj Ji Charan Singh, famous for initiating the largest number of seekers in the history of Radhasoami, told him that, as a student, he should first of all complete his studies before devoting his life to the divine path. Syd applied twice, and was twice rejected, perhaps because the guru could sense that Syd was unlikely to adhere to the cult's strict rules of vegetarianism and abstinence from alcohol and drugs. Syd, who was enormously interested in mysticism, was devastated.

Among the changing occupants of the various floors at Earlham Street were David Gale, and artist John Whiteley, a friend of Storm Thorgerson, who did the marbling on the front sleeve of *A Saucerful Of Secrets*. Also living there were Cambridge friends Sue Kingsford, whom Syd knew from Cambridge Tech, and her husband Jock. They were known as Mad Sue and Mad Jock Kingsford, a sobriquet given them for their zealous use of LSD. Syd persuaded his Cambridge girlfriend, fashion model Lynsey Korner, to come and live with him and, at least for a while, everything was looking good for Syd. The final occupant was Syd's new cat named Rover.

Syd's room was on the top floor, with access to the roof. He dragged a double mattress up the stairs and laid cheap straw matting. As was almost obligatory in those days, the bed was covered with an Indian print from Indiacraft which was also the source of the strings of beads and brass bells. There was a record player and a stack of albums: as American imports became available in 1966 he added *Freak Out*, the Mothers of Invention's first album, and *The Fugs* on ESP, both of which he bought at the Indica bookshop over at 102 Southampton Row who ordered them in from New York. Also among the albums were classic blues artists and rock including the Beatles, the Byrds, and Love. A large brown paper bag had been blown up to use as a lampshade, there was an easel erected by the window which faced north and a guitar

**Above:
A Saucerful Of
Secrets was
released in 1968.**

*As the paper had been raided on obscenity grounds by this time, her pubic hair was censored by more psychedelic squiggles to avoid another bust.

leaned against the wall; it was a classic bohemian pad. There was a cheap café just across Cambridge Circus at 20 Old Compton Street called the Pollo Bar and Restaurant (still there as this is written) where he took most of his meals and when the weather was fine he could sit on the flat roof and smoke a joint, strum his guitar and look out over the rooftops of Covent Garden as if he were in the Latin Quarter of Paris.

This was Syd's most creative period. Jenner told Robert Sandall: "The strongest image I always have of Syd is of him sitting in his flat in Earlham Street with his guitar and his book of songs, which he represented by paintings with different coloured circles. I was an immense Syd fan. You'd go round to Syd and you'd see him write a song. It just poured out." Wynne-Willson also remembers this as Syd's creative peak: "Those were halcyon days. He'd sit around with copious amounts of hash and grass and write these incredible songs. There's no doubt they were crafted very carefully and deliberately."

Whereas Syd began the year relatively straight, he was very undisciplined. His mother's pampering meant that he never placed any restraints on his behaviour, having always been told he was wonderful and special, so once he discovered the drug scene he jumped in feet first. Initially this only meant smoking pot, which he did a lot

of, often with Peter Jenner: 'None of them did drugs when I met them, except Syd, and he would only smoke dope. Then with the Summer Of Love and all that bollocks, Syd got very enthusiastic about acid, and got into the religious aspect of it, which I never did. The others were very straight. They were much more into half-a-pint of bitter than they were into drugs. One of the reasons I got on with Syd was because he and I used to smoke a lot of pot together. Rick would take a puff now and again, but Roger and Nick would never go near it. Syd was very much the artist, while the other two were the architects, and I think that's an important way of looking at what happened. Syd did this wild, impossible drawing, and they turned it into the Pink Floyd."

There is no doubt that Syd had a number of life-changing experiences at Earlham Street, mostly involving music, one of which is described by Alan Beam in his autobiography, *Rehearsal For The Year 2000* where Peter Wynne-Willson and Susie Gawler-Wright are known as John and Anne: "I went with John and Anne and half a dozen others to watch Handel's 'Messiah' at the Albert Hall with all of us tripping, having lined up beforehand to have two drops of LSD each on the tongue." For Willson it was "quite the most extraordinary thing I'd ever encountered," but Beam didn't fare so well: "On that trip I felt very miserable back at Earlham Street, and too shy to accept when Anne invited me to join them in drawing pictures on the wall." (This was a popular hippie activity; somewhat frowned upon by landlords).

Syd also liked to drop acid and play John Coltrane's 1965 masterpiece 'Om'. It was this type of intense musical experience he was hoping to create with his own ear-splitting feedback and chopped up time signatures. In many ways Syd was a precursor of the minimalist movement. He could have easily fitted in with future New York 'No Wave' guitarist Glenn Branca; as Andrew King stated, "Given the chance, Syd would have jammed the same chord sequence all night."

101 CROMWELL ROAD

There was no room to rehearse at Earlham Street or where Roger, Rick and Nick lived so band rehearsals were held at 101 Cromwell Road where Roger had lived after leaving Mike Leonard's flat. 101 was a regency building virtually next door to the West London Air Terminal where, in those days, you would check your luggage in before boarding an airline bus to London (Heathrow) Airport. 101 was a centre of underground activity, much of it to do with drugs. The ground floor flat was occupied by Nigel and Jenny Lesmoire-Gordon, friends of Syd's and Roger's from Cambridge who had moved to London in order for Nigel to become a film-maker. Living in a sort of hut constructed in their corridor was the poet John Esam, a tall, thin, spider-like New Zealander with jet black hair, slicked back like the wings of a beetle.

John was a great proselytizer of LSD – which was then still legal – and aside from Michael Hollingshead's World Psychedelic Centre in Pont Street, which had been set up by Timothy Leary John was the main source of acid in London. It was dangerous to visit his flat because people had been known to find themselves on a trip after eating an orange or drinking juice from the fridge; perhaps the origin of the stories that Syd's flatmates were feeding him acid. He certainly visited this flat a lot and eventually moved to a room upstairs in the building.

A friend of Esam's arrived from the States with several thousand trips for him, but had been followed by the police. John threw a bag of acid-laced sugar cubes into the garden but the police were waiting and caught it, expertly. The police arrested John but then found that LSD was still legal. In order to find a charge that would stick, they then claimed that the substance was ergot, the material acid is made from. They charged Esam under the Poisons Act (manufacturing poison carries an unlimited sentence) and the case went to the Old Bailey. The police were, in essence, trying to prove that LSD was ergot which as Steven Abrams – founder of the drugs research organisation SOMA – pointed out, was like saying that if you boiled instant orange juice, you would wind up with an orange. The prosecution brought over Dr. Albert Hoffman, the discoverer of LSD, from Basel to testify that LSD counted as ergot under the Poisons Act. Esam's team brought in Dr. Ernst B. Chain, the co-discoverer of penicillin with Sir Alexander Fleming, who maintained that LSD was not in fact made from organic ergotomine but a semi-synthetic derivative. The arguments were so complex that in the end the scientists got together in a huddle, told the judge to wait, and eventually concluded that LSD was not ergot and therefore John was innocent. The experience freaked Esam out to the extent that at least a decade passed before he would even smoke a joint.

At that time, one of the residents at 101 was the painter Duggie Fields. Though the flat's main connection was Cambridge through Nigel and Jenny, Roger Waters knew Duggie from the brief period Fields spent at the Regent Street Poly studying architecture before going on to the Chelsea School of Art in September 1964. It was probably through Roger that the Pink Floyd got to rehearse at 101 because he moved into part of the maisonette on the top two floors after leaving Mike Leonard's house in Highgate before finally moving on to live with his girlfriend in Shepherd's Bush.

Duggie Fields: "They used to rehearse in the flat and I used to go downstairs and put on Smokey Robinson as loud as possible. I don't know where they all arrived from, but I went to architecture school so did Rick and Roger. I don't quite remember how I met them all. I just remember suddenly being surrounded by the Pink Floyd and hundreds of groupies instantly."

The "hundreds of groupies" is something of an exaggeration; this didn't happen until the group began to play the UFO Club, but the high volume was certainly true. I remember visiting John Esam there at the time and we eventually had to go outside to a café in order to talk because the volume was so loud from their rehearsal that we couldn't hear each other speak.

THE IT LAUNCH PARTY AT THE ROUNDHOUSE
STRIP?????HAPPENINGS//////TRIP//////MOVIES
Bring your own poison & flowers & gas-filled balloons & submarine & rocket ship & candy & striped boxes & ladders & paint & flutes & ladders & locomotives & madness & autumn & blowlamps &
POP/OP/COSTUME/MASQUE/FANTASY/LOON/BLOWOUT/
DRAG BALL SURPRISE FOR THE SHORTEST/BAREST COSTUME.

The Albert Hall Beat poetry reading in the summer of 1965 had identified a community of like-minded people, many of them creative in one way or another, many of them interested in drugs, most of them young. Hoppy and I were very impressed with the energy and enthusiasm of these people and wondered what we could do to bring them together. We envisioned a newspaper, something along the likes of New York's *Village Voice* – there were no underground newspapers yet – and to this end Hoppy bought a sit-up-and-beg offset litho press and began experimenting with zinc plates. The flyers for the London Free School and the four issues of *The Grove*, the newspaper of the LFS were printed on this, as well as a literary magazine called *Long Hair* featuring a lengthy extract from Allen Ginsberg's journals (he also named the magazine).

Next we did something called the *Global Moon Edition Long Hair Times*, designed to be sold on the CND Aldermaston march of Easter 1966. It was simply stapled together like a poetry magazine but it was the forerunner of *International Times* (*IT*), the

'In fact it didn't even cover her bottom; this must have been the shortest of the evening, if not the barest.'

New Society

London underground newspaper – and the first underground newspaper in Europe – that Hoppy and I, and a dozen other people, published on October 14, that year.

IT was launched with a late night party on October 15, 1966, at the Roundhouse in Camden Town. This beautiful building originally housed the winding gear that pulled trains up the hill from Euston station but as soon as engines became more powerful it had had its day and became simply Engine Shed 1B. Gilby's Gin then used it as a bonded warehouse, constructing a giant circular wooden balcony to house the vats of gin, but by the time of the *IT* launch even this had become unsafe to walk on. The TUC Congress had passed a resolution to set up a workers arts centre, resolution 42, and playwright Arnold Wesker set up Centre 42 in order to create a workers paradise within the circular walls of the Roundhouse. But he first needed to raise about £380,000 to do it so the building sat cold and empty. *IT*'s accountant, Michael Henshaw, was also the accountant for Centre 42 and for Wesker himself. It was easy for him to get the keys and Wesker, thinking it was some form of book launch, wished us well.

The floor was thick with a century of dirt; in fact there may not even have been a proper floor, just equipment housings. Twisted iron jutted up from bits of broken concrete. People formed an enormous line outside; the only way in was up a very long narrow single-file staircase. It was so narrow that no-one could leave while other people were coming up, it was impossible to squeeze past. At the top, myself, Hoppy, and David Mairowitz handed out sugar cubes as we took the tickets. They were just sugar cubes but some people used them as an excuse to loosen up and dance wildly. You needed to because it was mid October and very cold. There was no heating and the Roundhouse was not insulated; the wind whistled beneath the loading doors onto the freight yards beyond. There were two lavatories which immediately flooded out, causing such huge puddles that the doors were removed and used as duck boards, and guards stood at the doors to shield the users from the gaze of the long queues waiting to wobble across the wonky boards. It was described in the press as a firetrap, but the main entrance was from the freight yards where there were several enormous doors for locomotives to get in. These were each manned, and were, of course, used by the bands to drive their vans in. We also had a medical doctor, Dr. Stuart Montgomery, publisher of the Fulcrum Press, on hand for emergencies.

There was a giant jelly that the Pink Floyd either did or did not run into with their van. I was there but I don't remember what happened; the most likely story is that Po, their roadie removed an important piece of wood to use in his setting up and the whole jelly, which was not yet perfectly set, tore loose from its tarpaulin mold. Daevid Allen described the launch as "one of the two most revolutionary events in the history of English alternative music and thinking. The *IT* event was important because it marked the first recognition of a rapidly spreading socio-cultural revolution that had its parallel in the States. It was its London newspaper. The New Year came... bringing and inexpressible feeling of change in the air." Daevid remembers two stages whereas there was not even one; the bands played from the bed of an old wooden horse wagon left behind by Gilby's Gin which had white sheeting draped behind it for the lightshow.

To emerge from the steep narrow staircase into the psychedelic light show that filled the dome of the Roundhouse with coloured blobs and patterns was an extraordinary experience. Binder, Edwards and Vaughan brought along their Fifties Cadillac painted in psychedelic patterns. Films by Kenneth Anger, William Burroughs and Antony Balch were projected on a sheet hanging from the balcony where the gin vats had been. Dutch couple Simon Postuma and Marijika Koger, later known as The Fool, told tarot cards in a fortune telling tent, from which billowed great gusts of incense. Paul McCartney wandered around dressed as an Arab to avoid recognition but, as the only Arab there, he inevitably attracted attention. *New Society* reported that Marianne Faithfull "was wearing what appeared to be a fair imitation of a nun's habit, which didn't quite make it to the ground: in fact it didn't even cover her bottom; this must have been the shortest of the evening, if not the barest."

Yes, she won the prize for the 'shortest/barest'. Michelangelo Antonioni (in

London to film *Blow Up*) and Monica Vitti in a stunning short white miniskirt turned people's heads. Kim Fowley explained to everyone how he had single-handedly started every band then playing on Sunset Strip. There were silver-foil headdresses, third-eye refraction lenses on foreheads, dragoon jackets and bondage gear and lots of glitter dust. The products of the Lebanese State Hashish factory were much in evidence. Soft Machine played first. Their line-up at that time was Daevid Allen (guitar), Kevin Ayers (bass), Mike Ratledge (organ) and Robert Wyatt (drums).

Daevid wrote: "That was our first gig as a quartet. Yoko Ono came on stage and created a giant happening by getting everybody to touch each other in the dark, right in the middle of the set. We also had a motorcycle brought onto stage and would put a microphone against the cylinder head for a good noise."

Then the Pink Floyd climbed onto the rickety old cart – it was all reminiscent of Elvis on the *Louisiana Hayride* – and their fans from the All Saints Hall gigs pushed the loon dancers out of the way to stand at the front. *IT* reported: "The Pink Floyd, psychedelic pop group, did weird things to the feel of the event with their scary feedback sounds, slide projections playing on their skin (drops of paint ran riot on the slides to produce outer-space/prehistoric textures on the skin), spotlights flashing in time with the drums." The majority of the audience had never seen a light show before and many stood staring open-mouthed as the amoeba-like bubbles of light pulsated and fused together in time to the music or expanded and blew apart into dozens of offspring.

The Floyd could not have had a more sympathetic audience and they responded with a brilliant set. The Roundhouse electricity supply was as decrepit as the rest of the building and when the Floyd cranked up the volume for the end of 'Interstellar Overdrive' they were suddenly plunged into darkness as the fuses blew, providing an unintentional but dramatic climax to their act. Light and sound was soon restored and I went to pay the groups for their fine work. I had to push my way through a crowd of fans, most of them converted in the last hour, before I could reach them. The Soft Machine received £12.10.0 and the Pink Floyd got £15.0.0 because they had a light show to pay for.

The poet Kenneth Rexroth, the poet, anarchist, scene-maker – he was the MC at the famous first reading of Ginsberg's *Howl* – was visiting from San Francisco and I had invited him along to the party. Sadly he mistook the Soft Machine for an audience jam session and may have even left before the Pink Floyd came on. He was terrified by the whole event and wrote an unintentionally funny report in his column in the *San Francisco Examiner*:

"The bands didn't show, so there was a large pickup band of assorted instruments on a small central platform. Sometimes they were making rhythmic sounds, sometimes not. The place is literally an old roundhouse, with the doors for the locomotives all boarded up and the tracks and turntable gone, but still with a dirt floor (or was it just very dirty?). The only lights were three spotlights. The single entrance and exit was through a little wooden door about three feet wide, up a narrow wooden stair, turning two corners, and along an aisle about two and a half feet wide made by nailing down a long table.

"Eventually about 3,500 people crowded past this series of inflammable obstacles. I felt exactly like I was on the Titanic. Far be it for me to holler copper, but I was dumbfounded that the police and fire authorities permitted even a dozen people to congregate in such a trap. Mary and I left as early as we politely could."

Hunter Davies in the *Sunday Times* reviewed the event with less concern for his own safety, providing the first national press for the Pink Floyd:

"At the launching of the new magazine *IT* the other night a pop group called the Pink Floyd played throbbing music while a series of bizarre coloured shapes flashed on a huge screen behind them. Someone had made a mountain of jelly and another person had parked his motor-bike in the middle of the room. All apparently very psychedelic...

"The group's bass guitarist, Roger Waters, [said] 'It's totally anarchistic. But it's co-operative anarchy if you see what I mean. It's definitely a complete realisation of the aims of psychedelia. But if you take LSD what you experience depends entirely on who you are. Our music may give you the screaming horrors or throw you into screaming ecstasy. Mostly it's the latter. We find our audiences stop dancing now. We tend to get them standing there totally grooved with their mouths open.' Hmmm."

The event has been described as the first ever 'rave'. It was a lot of fun and it launched IT on the London scene.

Above: Psychedelic debutante, Susie Gawler-Wright on the cover of International Times # 11, 1967.

CHAPTER SIX
UFO CLUB

CHAPTER SIX
UFO CLUB

IT almost immediately ran out of money and Hoppy decided to use the same formula that had provided funds for the London Free School to provide funds. The biggest challenge for *IT* was paying the staff wages so when he and Joe Boyd decided to start an underground club in the West End, it was agreed that the staff of *IT* would run it and be paid a high enough wage to make up for *IT*'s shortcomings. UFO Limited was a private company owned by Joe and Hoppy but it was generous in its support of the underground.

The UFO club – pronounced You-Fow – was the making of the Pink Floyd; this was where they were filmed by foreign crews, it was where journalists were invited to see them, and it was home to the greatest concentration of their fans, even though they played there only a handful of times. They were more or less unknown when UFO started, but were famous when it closed, less than a year later. At first Hoppy and Joe decided to try two gigs, one each side of Christmas, and if they were a success, to continue the event on a weekly basis. The Pink Floyd played at both events. UFO immediately became the *in* club of the London underground scene and the Pink Floyd its resident house band.

UFO was held every Friday night, all night, in the Blarney Club, an Irish Ballroom in a basement at 31 Tottenham Court Road featuring a distinctly Hibernian décor. The rent was only £15 for the night but because of the cinemas on the ground floor, no music was permitted until after 10pm. A wide, rather grand staircase led down to the ballroom to the left at the bottom, from which stray blobs of psychedelic light appeared to be escaping, as if oozing from the room. Halfway down the stairs, Mickey Farren, his hair a magnificent Afro, controlled the admission. As the club became very hot, the stairs were usually filled with people sitting on the steps, getting some air. It was a traditional ballroom, complete with a revolving mirror ball suspended from the ceiling – which the light show operators incorporated into their projections – and a polished dance floor. The only serious argument that the owner Mr. Gannon had with the organisers was when filmmaker Jack Henry Moore wanted to pile sand on the floor as part of an environmental happening. Apparently in the old days of cutthroat competition between ballroom owners, one of the ways of sabotaging a rival was to put sand on his dance floor.

Joe Boyd: "The object of the club is to provide a place for experimental pop music and also for the mixing of medias, light shows and theatrical happenings. We also show New York avant-garde films. There is a very laissez faire attitude at the club. There is no attempt made to make people fit into a formula, and this attracts the further out kids of London. If they want to lie on the floor they can, or if they want to jump on the stage they can, as long as they don't interfere with the group of course."

In addition to the bands, there was always a feature film – often a Marilyn Monroe

classic or Charlie Chaplin – and other, more experimental films screened by the
London Filmmakers Co-op such as films by Kenneth Anger, Andy Warhol from the
New York Cinematheque or Antony Balch and William Burroughs' *Towers Open Fire*.
UFO was known for its light shows which were not only directed at the band, but at all
the walls and ceiling to provide a total environment. Sometimes the films were used as
a part of multi-media events, such as the time when a modern jazz combo improvised
to old black and white Pathé newsreels.

Nick Mason: "It seems pretty strange, looking back on it – really hard to describe.
Endless rock groups, that's what 'underground' meant to the people, but that wasn't
what it really was. It was a mixture of bands, poets, jugglers and all sorts of acts."

Playwright David Z. Mairowitz, then working for *IT*, put on a weekly experimental
drama, like an underground soap opera, called 'The Flight Of The Erogenous' which
seemed to involve a lot of foam and paint being thrown about and female clothing
being removed. It always attracted a decent crowd. One week someone inflated a silver
weather balloon, and that bounced around the room for a while before being squeezed
through the double doors and up the stairs (inspiration for the Floyd's future flying
pigs?) The Giant Sun Trolley experimental sound/jazz group was a pickup band
created by the audience; it became Hydrogen Jukebox – named after the Allen
Ginsberg poem – and eventually the Third Ear Band.

Nick Mason told *Zigzag*: 'It [UFO] gets rosier with age, but there is a germ of truth
in it, because for a brief moment there looked as if there might actually be some

combining of activities. People would go down to this place and a number of people would do a number of things, rather than simply one band performing. There would be some mad actors, a couple of light shows, perhaps the recitation of some poetry or verse, and a lot of wandering about and a lot of cheerful chatter going on." In the early days, the Pink Floyd mingled with the crowd since it was more interesting than sitting backstage.

There was a food concession run by Greg Sams from the Praed Street macrobiotic restaurant and he did good business at three in the morning when everyone had the munchies. Greg also used the long nighttime hours to explain the ideas behind macrobiotics to his customers. Acid and pot was easily obtainable from any number of dealers including the large German dealer Manfred, who apparently always gave away his first 400 trips. Tony Smythe from the Council for Civil Liberties was always on hand, usually conducting meetings in a back room, in case the police decided to raid and of course Michael X used it as a place to relive white liberals of guilt money by getting people to contribute to his – largely fictitious – projects in the Black Community. *International Times* was on sale and other underground publications. The Kings Road clothes shops Granny Takes A Trip, Hung On You and Dandy Fashions, were always represented in case anyone fancied ordering a frilly shirt or a pair of yellow crushed velvet loon pants.

The UFO audience arrived in their psychedelic finery: shimmering silver micro-mini-skirts contrasted with full length granny dresses in silk or chiffon; revamped negligees worn as tops, velvet jackets, shirts with huge lapels and frilly fronts in tasteful paisley or Liberty flower pattern prints. The local police never really got the hang of the new Sixties clothes and hairstyles. One time they spotted someone entering the club whose description matched that of a 16-year old runaway girl. Half way to Tottenham Court Road police station, a block away, they discovered they had seized a young man. In the early days they were friendly, and one telephone call from them ran as follows:

"We've got one of yours 'ere. Wot shall we do wiv 'im?"

Mickey Farren, having seen an acid crazed hippie, eyes ablaze, refractive lens in the middle of his forehead, flash past him up the stairs and heading in the direction of the police station: "Just hang onto 'im. We'll send someone up to get 'im."

There was dancing at the UFO, but usually to records: 'Granny Takes A Trip' by the Purple Gang and 'My White Bicycle' by Tomorrow, became perennial favourites and when a band was on, most people sat and listened. There were loon dancers near the front, but most of the audience sat on the floor, which, according to Robert Wyatt, was very conducive to good playing:

"One of the biggest influences was the atmosphere at UFO. In keeping with the general ersatz orientalism of the social setup you'd have an audience sitting down... Just the atmosphere created by an audience sitting down was very inductive to playing, as in Indian classical music, a long droning introduction to a tune. It's quite impossible if you've got a room full of beer swigging people standing up waiting for action, it's very hard starting with a drone. But if you've got a floor full of people, even the few that are listening, they're quite happy to wait for a half hour for the first tune to get off the ground."

Long improvisations were needed in long sets and were easier if you were playing experimental or freeform music; when the Beatles were on stage for eight hours a night in Hamburg, they developed a 30 minute version of Ray Charles' 'What'd I Say?' to fill the time. As far as the Soft Machine were concerned it was a practical response to the stage situation: Mike Ratledge's Lowry Holiday Deluxe organ had a tendency to feedback during pauses if the volume was very high – as it always was at UFO – which prompted a style of continuous playing since they couldn't stop.

Announcements at UFO were usually more along the lines of the page headings in *International Times* intoned by Jack Henry Moore in his campy Southern accent: "If you can't turn your parents on, turn on them" or "Maybe tonight is kissing night. Don't just kiss your lover tonight, kiss your friends". Richard Neville called UFO "traumatic, familial, euphoric" and described it as "the Underground's living equivalent to *The Times* letters column." Whenever anything happened that affected the scene, everyone gathered at UFO to discuss it: when the police busted *International Times*, it was at UFO that the latest issue was read aloud from the manuscripts which had been quickly hidden in Indica Bookshop on the ground floor; when Hoppy was jailed for a small amount of pot, all manner of incendiary responses to his incarceration were proposed at that week's UFO; and when Mick Jagger and

Above: UFO Club posters by Michael English and Nigel Waymouth.

Keith Richards were sentenced to prison after the *News of the World* set them up for a police bust, it was from UFO that people set off to hold a midnight demonstration outside that newspaper's Fleet Street headquarters; probably the first night-time demonstration Britain had ever known.

In addition to the Pink Floyd, the Crazy World of Arthur Brown and the Soft Machine were also regarded as house bands at UFO. Arthur Brown was tall and lanky and pre-figured Kiss by painting his face into a crazy mask for each performance. He always entered wearing a flaming head-dress which more than once had to be put out with a pint of beer emptied over his head when his cloak caught fire as he dipped and dived; he was an energetic dancer and really knew how to get the audience going. (The beer came from backstage; there was no alcohol sold at UFO). Pete Townshend, who was a regular at UFO, recognised his talent and got him signed to Track, the Who's new label.*

For a while it seemed that the Soft Machine were the Grateful Dead to the Pink Floyd's Jefferson Airplane (or vice versa); these two underground groups came from similar middle class backgrounds – Canterbury and Cambridge – and played to the same underground audience. They shared the bill at the launch party of *International Times*, and if the Floyd were in on the origins of UFO, members of the Soft Machine were involved with the people who created *International Times* from as far back as 1964. Nonetheless, it was only Daevid Allen who really fitted in.

Robert Wyatt: "We felt like suburban fakes dressed up on Saturday and visiting the city. I never dared take LSD. I was in total awe of the audience at UFO, people like the *Oz* crowd. We used to come in on the train and pretend we were like them. Just because we played long solos people assumed we were stoned, which was great for our credibility. I didn't know much about it. Daevid had connections with a whole generation of people there, all these people with very advanced ideas. Daevid was the internationalist of the group, he got us into all of that. The rest of us were all provincial."

Daevid's connections went right back to the Beat Hotel in Paris, when he took over Allen Ginsberg's room in 1958 after the poet returned to New York. Daevid, known as a poet back then, knew many of the early experimenters with LSD, having first taken it in 1960 so it was almost inevitable that his band – named after one of William Burroughs' books – should become a UFO regular. It was a short lived season because in August 1967 British customs refused to let Daevid back into the country after a French tour on the grounds that he had overstayed his visa the last time he entered. Soft Machine was reduced to a trio and Daevid went to Paris and started Gong.

At the time Soft Machine had the best light show in Britain as Daevid explained in his book *Gong Dreaming*: "The light show we used for our UFO gigs was run by Mark Boyle, a Scottish sculptor turned liquid lightshow alchemist. The combinations of liquids he sandwiched between the twin glass lenses, that began to alter as they were heated by the projector lamp, were his professional secret. He worked inside a tent so nobody could see what he was doing. Some said he used his own fresh sperm mixed with the colours and other liquids and fluids. He felt a special affinity for our music and although it could not be logically programmed, his lights synchronised with our stops, starts, peaks, and lows, as if it had all been pre-organised by a wizardly Atlantean reincarnate."

Mark Boyle had evolved his early light show at Mike Leonard's Sound/Light workshop at Hornsey Art College, the same place that Joey Gannon's ideas were developed. Boyle operated the stage lights and sometimes played tricks on the bands, like making green bubbles emerge from their tightly stretched flies – a trick he liked to play on Roger Waters – but he was only one of many lightshow operators and the Floyd usually had their own spectacular show. The blobs and bubbles of the lights were absorbed into each other or divided like the school diagrams of amoebas. One's whole vision was filled with pulsating cellular forms, like being inside a plant or your own body, the sap rushing, being borne along by the relentless rhythm. People sometimes just stood open mouthed.

UFO had a number of different light shows in simultaneous operation including one by Jack Braclin's Fireacre Lights that had played at the London Free School. Fiveacres was his psychedelic nudist colony near Watford, which consisted mostly of local teachers living in caravans. The wooden clubhouse had a 'trip machine' consisting of an electrically powered wheel on the ceiling from which strips of silver Mellonex hung down to the floor. As the wheel slowly turned, the assembled tripping nudists watched the flashing colours to the accompaniment of a very scratched copy

*Pete and his manager Kit Lambert produced Arthur's single, 'Fire', which went to number one in August 1968.

of Zappa's *Freak Out*. The Pink Floyd played there on November 5, 1966, Guy Fawkes Night – stopping off to see the fireworks on their way back to London from a concert at Wilton Hall, Bletchley.

At UFO Jack sometimes projected on to the bands, as he had done at the LFS, but mostly kept one end of the large room fully filled with moving blobs and white dots. Jack's lights were some of the best in town, and he soon set up his own weekly nightclub called Happening 44, at 44 Gerrard Street in Soho which on other nights was a seedy strip club. Jack had first developed his light shows for patients at mental hospitals where the patients would first listen to some records and be given a cup of coffee. This was followed by an hour of slide projections.

According to Alph Moorcroft the best of these was made by a girl patient at Knapsbury mental hospital: "The slides consisted of bright heaving masses of colour and produced amazing emotional reactions, tears and often a state of disturbance which lasted for days. Because of these reactions some of the hospitals he visited decided that his shows were 'too loaded' emotionally and therefore stopped them." The effect at UFO was sometimes equally hypnotic and people danced for hours surrounded by the swirling shapes and points of light.

A wide variety of bands performed at UFO: Procol Harum played their second ever gig there and their fourth (by which time they were already at number one with 'A Whiter Shade Of Pale'); the Move made an attempt at underground credibility by playing but the UFO audience didn't like their mohair suits and aggressive act and booed them. The rest of the country, however, seemed convinced by their nods to flower power such as 'I Can Hear The Grass Grow' and 'Flowers In The Rain.' The latter was the first single to be played on BBC's new Radio 1 pop channel but the publicity campaign, consisting of a postcard involving a drawing of the prime minister Harold Wilson naked in the bath assisted by his secretary, attracted a winning libel suit and they group forfeited their royalties from this, one of their biggest hits. Jimi Hendrix, whose manager, Chas Chandler now also managed the Soft Machine, used to come down in the early hours and jam with whoever was on stage. Sadly these were

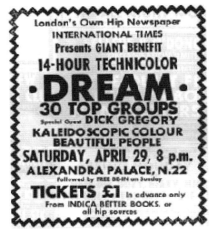

> '**Yeah, sometimes, we just sorta let loose a bit and started hitting the guitar a bit harder and not worrying quite so much about the chords.**'
>
> *Syd Barrett*

never recorded but to those of us who witnessed them, they are among the high spots of the Sixties.

HOUSE BAND TO THE UNDERGROUND

More than anything else, the UFO club remains synonymous with the Pink Floyd's rise to fame. By now Syd had permed his hair into a Hendrix Afro – as did Eric Clapton and many other musicians – and was dressed in silks and satins and flowing scarves from Thea Porter, Granny Takes A Trip and Hung On You. Roger Waters and the others always looked vaguely uncomfortable in hippie clothing, particularly when Roger appeared with what looked like a pelmet sewn to the bottom of his trouser legs. The idea of Roger perming his hair was unthinkable, but Syd not only looked the part but was himself a sartorial inspiration to the next generation: people like Marc Bolan modelled themselves on Syd and his Vidal Sassoon perm.

When the Floyd took the stage, and began the familiar descending cadence of bass notes that led to 'Interstellar Overdrive' the hippies sitting out on the stairs would rush the doors to get in and the crowd on the dance floor would push forward. The group talked about the dancing in an early interview for Canadian Broadcasting Corporation (CBC). Canadian scriptwriter and film-maker Nancy Bacal, who studied at the Royal Academy of Music and Dramatic Art (RADA) was producing radio shows for CBC. At that time she was living with Michael de Freitas (Michael X) who soon introduced her to the London Free School scene. In January 1967 she made a programme about the newly emergent London underground scene for CBC and interviewed Nick Mason, Roger Waters and Syd Barrett. In doing so, Bacal inadvertently taped one of the very few surviving recordings of Barrett talking about his music and the band.

Nancy Bacal: "In a frenetic haze of sound and sight, a new concept of music has begun to penetrate the senses of Britain's already hopped-up beat fans. Some call it free sound, others prefer to include it in the psychedelic wave of 'isms' already circulating around the Western hemisphere. But this music, here and now, is that of the Pink Floyd, a group of four young musicians, a light man, and an array of equipment sadistically designed to shatter the strongest nerves."

At first Nick demurred, telling her: "We didn't start out trying to get anything new... We originally started virtually as an R&B group."

Syd: "Yeah, sometimes, we just sorta let loose a bit and started hitting the guitar a bit harder and not worrying quite so much about the chords."

Roger: "It stopped being third rate academic rock, y'know? It started being a sort of intuitive groove, really."

Nick: "It's free-form. In terms of construction it's almost like jazz, where you start off with a riff and then you improvise on this except..."

Roger: "Where it differs from jazz is that if you're improvising around a jazz number, if it's a 16 bar number you stick to 16 bar choruses and you take 16 bar solos, whereas with us it starts and we may play three choruses of something that lasts for 17 and a half bars each chorus and then it'll stop happening and it'll stop happening when it stops happening *and* it may be 423 bars later or four."

Syd: "And it's not like jazz music 'cause..."

Nick: "We all want to be pop stars – we don't want to be jazz musicians."

Syd: "Exactly. And I mean we play for people to dance to – they don't seem to dance much now but that was the initial idea. So we play loudly and we're playing with electric guitars, so we're utilising all the volume and all the effects you can get. But now in fact we're trying to develop this by using the lights."

Roger: "But the thing about the jazz thing is that we don't have this great musician thing. Y'know, we don't really look upon ourselves as musicians as such, y'know, period... reading the dots, all that stuff."

Nancy asked how important the visual aspect of the production was and they all agreed it was very important...

Syd: "It's quite a revelation to have people operating something like lights while

you're playing as a direct stimulus to what you're playing. It's rather like audience reaction except it's sort of on a higher level, you know, you can respond to it and then the lights will respond back..."

During the early UFO period, the band was Syd's: he was the lead singer, lead guitarist and group songwriter. Just as later his illness meant that he was no longer wholly present, in the early days he was 100% there, totally involved, giving everything to the music. As the lead singer he was the only one to attract attention from the audience; because the band was obscured by the light show the Pink Floyd were never famous in the usual rock star sense and even at the height of their fame they were able to walk the streets and go to shops without anyone knowing who they were. Syd, however, enjoyed fame and made sure that the girls up front could see him in his Hendrix afro and his Kings Road psychedelic finery.

The nature of Syd's songs – often in the first person – also demanded that the audience knew who was singing them. Syd's lyrics were very much of the zeitgeist: Keith West, the Incredible String Band, Fairport Convention, the Kinks and many other bands including the Beatles were singing about English subject matter in an English accent instead of the imitation American accents and pseudo-American themes that had previously dominated the charts. Barrett's songs were those of a clever middle class schoolboy. If Mary Tourtel's cartoon creation Rupert Bear took acid and wrote rock songs they would be like Syd Barrett's efforts: lines and images from Hilaire Belloc whom Syd adored, particularly from his nonsense verse; names and images from Tolkien's *Lord Of The Rings*; from Edward Lear; from Kenneth Grahame's *Wind In The Willows*; Lewis Carroll's *Alice* books; folk tales of the Cambridgeshire fens; bits of Shakespeare; bits from Christopher Smart's 'Jubilate' (his 'My Cat Geoffrey' also influenced Allen Ginsberg); a collage of whatever was in the papers, overheard conversation, friend's names, everyday life. His girlfriends also inspired lines in his Floyd songs; Jenny Spires appeared as "Jennifer Gentle, she's a witch" in 'Lucifer Sam', Lynsey Korner was described as "Cornering neatly, she trips up sweetly" in 'Apples And Oranges'. Anything and everything went in.

The songs caught the spirit of the time, they had an innocence, a sweetness, a poignancy, and an evocation of childhood that was very appealing. Syd's lyrics connected directly to shared British memories of fairytales, of Hobbits, of going down the rabbit hole, Rupert Bear being called home for tea by his mother standing at the gate; unflappable Professor Quatermass seemingly unperturbed that one of his astronauts has been somehow absorbed by the other in a cheap soundstage made from a garden shed; square-jawed Dan Dare confronting the aliens each week in the *Eagle*; Flash Gordon bumping around a cheap interplanetary set in a rocketship that burned like a damp firework in search of aliens with angel wings; Syd and Rick's bleeps and squeals like the scary BBC Radiophonic Workshop soundtrack to the *Red Planet* radio serial; the boy at school with a scared mouse in his pocket; Uncle Mac and BBC *Childrens' Hour*; Christopher Robin; the excitement at first hearing rock 'n' roll washing in on waves of static from Luxembourg; it was all there.

**Above:
5th Dimension,
Leicester; UFO
Club and Saville
Theatre posters
by Michael
English and Nigel
Waymouth.**

Though they seem to have a string element of spontaneous, stream-of-consciousness rambling to them, Peter Jenner says that Syd drew his songs on paper like the overlapping circles of Venn diagrams, carefully planning the images and their relationship. All of this was in direct contrast to the music; though he was capable of well-crafted, pop melodies such as 'Arnold Layne' and 'See Emily Play', his musical interests lay in exploring the outer limits of sound production: feedback – then still a new thing – detuning and retuning the guitar strings during the performance, or by creating screeches, blips, insect clicks and metallic shrieks by running his Zippo lighter up and down the strings and manipulating his Binson Echorec, all in the best Keith Rowe manner. It was this aspect of Barrett's playing that provides continuity within the complete oeuvre of the Pink Floyd; they did not jump straight from jolly pop songs to long meandering improvisations. In the beginning they had both and they sat in uneasy opposition to each other until the pop songs were jettisoned.

The extended improvisations were much appreciated at UFO and hardly liked at all in most other venues. Even at UFO it must be said that the Floyd could actually be pretty boring after a while because they were not accomplished musicians and though the loon dancers and Nick Mason's drumming kept it going, Syd often ran out of ideas on long pieces as he fooled with his Binson Echorec and tried to come up with something new. Nick always reminded me of Chico Hamilton in *Jazz On A Summer's Day* with his muted mallets, steadfastly keeping the number alive while Syd turned his

Right:
The poster for the first UFO/ Nite Tripper club event, designed by

Michael English and featuring model Karen Astley, Pete Townshend's girlfriend.

knobs and fumbled with the machine head.

Nick: "We could only play in London, because there the audience was more tolerant and was willing to withstand 10 minutes of shit to discover five minutes of good music. We were at an experimental stage. We set out for unbelievable solos where no one else would dare."

Rick: "The band was an improvising group in the beginning. A lot of rubbish came out of it but a lot of good too. A lot of that was obviously to do with Syd – that was the way he worked. Then things got a lot more structured when Dave joined. He was a fine guitarist, but he wasn't really comfortable with all that wild psychedelic stuff."

Rick was the only really competent player: Nick did a good job on time keeping but rarely strayed from familiar time signatures. Syd had a fairly rudimentary knowledge of lead guitar, preferring the expedient of making abstract sounds with his instrument rather than astonishing the girls with tricky chords and difficult solos. Roger was never interested in expressing himself by becoming an adept instrumentalist – in fact Rick used to have to tune his bass for him because he was tone deaf.

Waters told the BBC: "There was a need to experiment in order to find another way of expressing ourselves that didn't involve practicing playing guitar for 10 years. At that time people were standing there in little suits with Gibsons and bass guitars held against the chest... and although it wasn't very complicated stuff it wasn't something I was interested in doing. In fact if you turned the thing up loud and used a plectrum – and I had a Rickenbacker which I bought with a grant, in fact my entire terms grant – if you banged it hard it made strange noises and I found if you pushed the strings against the pick-ups, it made a funny clicking noise."

GROUPIE STATUS

It was at UFO that Jenny Fabian first saw the Pink Floyd whom she dubbed Satin Odyssey in her lightly fictionalised roman-a-clef *Groupie*. "They were the first group to open people up to sound and colour, and I took my first trip down there when the *Satin* were playing, and the experience took my mind right out and I don't think it came back the same.' She was going out with Andrew King, renamed Nigel Bishop in her book, but it was Syd, whom she calls Ben, she really desired.

"He was tall and thin, and his eyes had the polished look I'd seen in other people who had taken too many trips in too short a time. I found him completely removed from the other three in the group; he was very withdrawn and smiled a lot to himself."

Inevitably she lured him into her bedroom and the breathless reader knows exactly what is going to happen when "Finally Ben reached down and untied his gymshoes..." As Syd later said, "Everything was so rosy at UFO. It was really nice to go there after slogging around the pubs and so on. Everyone had their own thing."

The audience wore lace and crushed velvet and the women found antique granny dresses, see-through tops or mico-mini dresses printed in psychedelic patterns. There were kaftans and bells – DJ John Peel always looked faintly embarrassed by his kaftan – and bare feet which gave a distinct aroma to the room. Many of them seemed very young and vulnerable and the staff felt very protective toward them; one of the rooms backstage was used to talk people down from bad trips. There was a man with long hair and a thick afghan coat who stood on a chair to the left of the stage each week who appeared to be unaffected by the fact that the temperature was about 90 degrees, and another who always brought his skinny dog with him who objected violently when animal loving hippies suggested that the high volume and heat might be bad for the poor animal's health.

Rock stars like Paul McCartney could come and sit in the dust and listen to the music like anyone else and not be bothered. Some, like Pete Townshend, were regulars and saw themselves as part of the scene. The girl with 'UFO' painted across her face by Michael English on the first UFO poster was Pete's girlfriend and future wife Karen Astley. He remembered dancing on acid to the Pink Floyd:

"I remember being in the UFO club with my girlfriend, dancing under the influence of acid. My girlfriend used to go out with no knickers and no bra on, in a dress that looked like it had been made out of a cake wrapper, and I remember a bunch of mod boys, still doing leapers, going up to her, and literally touching her up while she was dancing and she didn't know that they were doing it. I was just totally lost: she's there going off into the world of Roger Waters and his impenetrable leer, and there's my young lads coming down to see what's happening: 'Fuckin' hell, there's Pete Townshend, and he's wearing a dress.'"

Though the audience usually sat for the Pink Floyd, there were a certain number who danced: one or two who were proficient in proper loon dancing braved the front of the stage, but most of them writhed about to the right of the stage. In her CBC interview Nancy Bacal asked the band if their audiences danced. "They may dance," Nick told her. "It depends on the sort of music and what's happening."

Syd: "Yeah and anyway you hardly ever get the sort of dancing right from the beginning that you get just as a response to the rhythm. Usually people stand there and if they... [*laughs*] get into some sort of hysteria while they're there..."

Nick: "...the dancing takes the form of a frenzy which is very good."

Roger: "They don't all stand in a line and do the Madison. The audiences tend to be standing there and just one or two people maybe will suddenly flip out and rush forward and start leaping up and down..."

Syd: "Freak out I think is the word, you're looking for!"

Nick: "It's an excellent thing because this is what dancing is..."

Syd: "This is *really* what dancing is!"

UFO was also a useful showcase for the Pink Floyd so that music business people could catch their act.

John Peel: "The first time I ever saw them was at the old UFO club in Tottenham Court Road, where all of the hippies used to put on Kaftans and bells and beads and go and lie on the floor in an altered condition and listen to whatever was going on." The Floyd's appearances on Peel's influential *Top Gear* show were very important to their career.

Perhaps another reason why the UFO has become so legendary is because it produced the only English equivalent of the American Family Dog and Bill Graham posters. Most were done by Michael English and Nigel Waymouth, operating under the name of Hapshash and the Coloured Coat, a derivative of the Egyptian Queen Hatshepsut who organised the legendary journey to Punt, only changed to incorporate the word 'hash'. These were published by the equally faux Egyptian Osiris Visions Limited poster company owned by Joe Boyd, which quickly branched out and began making posters for other venues such as Brian Epstein's Saville Theatre, for record companies, art galleries and boutiques. The posters were silk-screened by hand, and often incorporated exquisite rainbow effects, running from silver to gold, or orange to yellow.*

Unfortunately, UFO articles in the *Sunday Times* and *Financial Times*, as well as the music weeklies, attracted the attention of the gutter press and *The People* sent an undercover reporter down to sniff out some dirt. Their man reported observing someone smoking a joss-stick – whatever that means – and even saw a couple kissing. Though the article was mild by Fleet Street's muck-raking standards it was enough to alert the police. The uneasy truce that had existed between Tottenham Court Road police station and the UFO management came to an end. The police used their usual tactics and threatened to rescind the Blarney Club's drinks licence, even though no alcohol was served at UFO. Mr. Gannon had no choice but to ask UFO to leave, but not before he revealed that he had been offered quite a large sum of money by one of the Fleet Street Sundays to spill the beans on the hippies. Brian Epstein offered the use of the Saville Theatre, but Joe Boyd and Hoppy decided that the Roundhouse, where it had all started, was a more appropriate venue.

Centre 42 had been astonished when *IT* used the Roundhouse for a party and realised that they had been missing out on a way of raising funds; they brought the place up to fire and health regulation standards and began renting it as a venue. By the time UFO moved there the Roundhouse was now in much better condition, with toilets and a proper entrance. In fact, even before UFO began, the Pink Floyd had returned to the Roundhouse for something called 'Psychodelphia Versus Ian Smith. Giant Freak Out' on December 3, where the audience was encouraged to "bring your own happenings and ecstatogenic substances." The Ian Smith in question was the pro-apartheid right-winger who had declared independence from British rule for Rhodesia and who was depicted on the poster for the event – which was organised by the Majority Rule for Rhodesia Committee – with his face annotated to look like that of Hitler with the moustache and cowlick.

Naturally this interested the *Daily Telegraph* who demanded to know what "ecstatogenic substances" were. Organiser Roland Muldoon told them they were "Anything which produces ecstasy in the body. Alcohol was not allowed for the rave-up, unhappily, and nor were drugs... All it means really is that you should bring your own bird."

Fleet Street never fully understood what the Sixties were all about.

*Many of the early ones were never reprinted and are consequently very rare and expensive collectors' items.

CHAPTER SEVEN
FROM ARNOLD
TO EMILY

CHAPTER SEVEN
FROM ARNOLD
TO EMILY

By the end of 1966, the band's academic studies were being seriously affected by their workload: they played gigs on October 31, November 4, 5 (two different venues), 8, 15, 18, 19, 22... The members began to think seriously about whether to turn professional or cut back and continue with their education; clearly they could not do both. They had virtually committed themselves to giving it a try when they signed a six-way partnership deal with Peter Jenner and Andrew King on October 31 and all became members of the six-way partnership Blackhill Enterprises.

Until that point they had played to largely sympathetic audiences. Had they known what their reception would be like out in the provinces they might have reconsidered and decided that architecture and the arts were not so bad after all. However this was to come later, when the group was being booked on the strength of a chart single. At first they were favoured with supportive audiences and often ideal settings. One such was their 'Music In Colour' concert, held at the Commonwealth Institute in Kensington on January 17, 1967. Jenner's new wife Sumi worked as an assistant to classical music promoter Christopher Hunt who, at her insistence, went to see the Pink Floyd play. He was favourably impressed and decided to book them.

Hunt: "I like what they do. I usually deal with classical chamber music but I believe that the Pink Floyd are something different from normal pop music. In fact, I have no interest at all in any other pop groups." It was a beautiful event, attracting a UFO-style audience as well as the type of person normally seen at concerts of Berg, Schoenberg or Stravinsky. A successful concert in such a prestigious venue inevitably pushed them further towards turning professional. They really had to make up their minds; something that, as a band, they were bad at doing. Nick was still working in his father-in-law's office, Rick was attending music classes, and Syd still sometimes turned up at Camberwell. Roger had the worst of it as he was trying to hold down a day job as an architect getting work experience at Fitzroy Robinson and Partners where he was engaged in designing bank vaults for the Bank of England. No wonder he was able to later write so convincingly about 'Money'.

Peter and Andrew took the group into the Thompson Private Recording Company in Hemel Hempstead to record a demo tape to be sent around the record companies, a la the Beatles. But when the tape was played to Joe Boyd, the only person that any of them knew in the music business, he told them that the recording quality was dreadful and that they should spend more money in recording the songs professionally, then the record companies would have a ready-made product that they could release. This made sense, except that recording sessions were costly and funds were low. By a stroke of good fortune, the film-maker Peter Whitehead had been having an affair with Jenny Spires, Syd's Cambridge girlfriend before Lynsey Korner.

**Below: Rick
Wright at one
with the cosmos.**

When Peter was commissioned to make a film about 'Swinging London' by the British Film Institute, she asked him to include Syd's band in it and, as he was feeling guilty about seeing her behind Syd's back, he agreed to finance a recording session and to film it.

Jenner and King asked Boyd if he would produce the session. Joe had recently recorded an album with the Incredible String Band, whom he both produced and managed through his new company Witchseason Productions – named after a line in Donovan's 'Season Of The Witch': "Beatniks out to make it rich" – and had used Sound Techniques, a four-track facility at 46a Old Church Street, Chelsea (conveniently close to the Chelsea Arts Club). The recording engineer at Sound Techniques, John Wood, was particularly good at getting an accurate reproduction of sound – much needed with the ISB's bells and whistles and wavering vocals – and the room had a very good feel to it. Before the sessions, the Floyd went down to watch AMM record there in order to familiarise themselves with the room and to see how a recording session actually worked. Peter Whitehead paid £80 to the band for the rights to use the results in his film and at eight in the morning of January 11, 1967 the Pink Floyd began their first proper studio session. They recorded 'Interstellar Overdrive' and 'Nick's Boogie' both of which are now on the DVD *Pink Floyd London 1966/1967*.[*] That afternoon, and the next were spent making mono mixes of the tapes. John Wood got a very rich sound and this is easily the best recording of the first Pink Floyd line-up in full improvisational mode.

*There are, in fact, no 1966 tracks on the release.

Boyd, in his capacity as UK representative of Jac Holzman's Elektra Records, initially wanted to sign them to Elektra, but Holzman only saw the Floyd in rehearsal and got no idea of the excitement they generated live – which a good producer can of course capture in a studio – so he passed. Joe's next idea was to approach Hort Schmolzi at Polydor, who was just opening up in Britain and had negotiated territorial distribution deals which got him the Who, Cream, and the Jimi Hendrix Experience. Schmolzi expressed an interest and the Floyd were booked into Polydor's Stratford Place studios to rehearse for recording 'Arnold Layne', as well to see if the facilities were good enough to record in if the deal with Polydor went through.

In the meantime, booking agent Bryan Morrison heard the buzz that the Floyd was creating and booked them into the Architectural Association, even though he had never heard them. Always on the look out for the next big thing, he showed up at Polydor's studios, accompanied by his assistants Tony Howard and Steve O'Rourke, to watch them rehearse. Unlike their own hippie managers, these were real music business types in camel-hair coats, short hair and Italian Mafia style suits. Joe was horrified because Morrison immediately launched into hard nose music biz talk. He airily dismissed the Polydor deal and said that they could get far more from EMI.

Joe Boyd: "I was theoretically going to be their record producer and we had a deal with Polydor. Then their agents told them they would make more, they would get a bigger advance, if they made the record first and sold the master to EMI. And ultimately this was true. They got offered a £5,000 advance from EMI, whereas they would have had a £1,000-£1,500 advance off Polydor but the royalty rate would have been much higher."

Morrison said he would finance recording of the single in return for the publishing and Boyd was asked to produce it. In vain Joe asked for a commitment to produce an album but they argued this would tie their hands in negotiating with EMI who were notoriously anti-freelance producers and always liked to use their own in-house men.[*] Even though he was being asked to sabotage his own deal with Polydor, Boyd agreed to do it because he thought that if 'Arnold Layne' was a hit, they would be foolish to use anyone else to produce the album.

'Arnold Layne' and it's B-side 'Candy And A Currant Bun' were recorded at Sound Techniques on January 29, 1967; eight or more takes for 'Arnold' and only two for 'Candy'. It took another day, or maybe two, to mix down to mono from the four-track masters. The instrumental solo on 'Arnold' was quite tricky and took some time to get right, requiring some nimble work with the faders: Roger helped Joe pull tracks in and out. Boyd and engineer John Woods excelled themselves.

Nick Mason: "I think we started to develop a cult following because everyone was talking about the psychedelic revolution and light and sound and all the rest of it. People were looking to try and guess, as they always are, what was going to happen next in music. This suddenly looked like what was going to happen next. I mean, we were incredibly awful, we were a dreadful band, we must have sounded frightful, but we were so different and so odd that I think – I mean odd, for those days. Of course, now, people would look at it and laugh. You look at the early photographs and we just look like a sort of elderly version of the Monkees or something. At the time, that was what was happening and no-one really understood it, but they all thought they ought to try and get in on it. So the record deal was in fact a really rather good one considering we had no track record whatsoever and couldn't play the instruments."

As Joe feared would happen, he got shafted. He told me in 1980: "My only deal was to get a royalty on 'Arnold Layne' which, by the way, I've never gotten, because the contract ended up in the hands of Blackhill Enterprises... Basically what happened was that EMI said, 'We'll give you this contract and £5,000 and we want you to use our studios and our staff producers and everything.' So they immediately went in and said, 'Thanks a lot for doing 'Arnold Layne,' Joe. See you around,' and at the time I didn't really fight it. I didn't really know what to do about it. Well, you know, it's up to the group. If the group felt strongly enough that they wanted me to be their record producer they would have insisted on me to EMI, so ultimately it's not really a business thing..."

Within the underground community there was enormous sympathy with Joe and many people felt that the Floyd had sold out. This was the reason that the Flies yelled 'Sell out' at them from the side of the stage at UFO; not because they'd signed to EMI but because they had not insisted on Boyd as their producer.[*]

The original idea, as proposed by Bryan Morrison, was to record six songs and choose the best two to hawk around the record companies. 'Arnold Layne' was not the

band's first choice for a single.

Nick Mason: "We really didn't want 'Arnold Layne' to be our first single... We recorded the first two and they were snatched away and we were told 'That's it!' All the record companies wanted the disc, so it was just a case of holding out for the biggest offer. By the time 'Arnold Layne' was released, we had already progressed and changed our ideas about what a good hit record should be. We tried to stop it being released but we couldn't."

'Arnold Layne' had a mildly fetishistic story line based on someone who stole girls' underwear from washing lines. 'Both my mother and Syd's mother had students as lodgers," said Roger in a 1967 interview, "because there was a girls' college up the road. So there were constantly great lines of bras and knickers on our washing lines, and Arnold, or whoever he was, had bits and pieces off our washing lines. They never caught him. He stopped doing it after a bit when things got too hot for him. Maybe he's moved to Cherry Hinton or Newnham possibly."

The underwear thief became notorious and Roger made sure to keep Syd informed of the latest gossip. Syd was amused by the story and during his frequent hour-long train journeys between Cambridge and London, he wrote a song about it. It took him three weeks and became the jump-off point for a long improvisation in the Floyd's set.

Syd: "Well I just wrote it. I thought 'Arnold Layne' was a nice name, and it fitted very well into the music I had already composed. I was at Cambridge at the time. I started to write the song. I pinched the line about "moonshine washing line" from Rog, our bass guitarist - because he has an enormous washing line in the back of his house. Then I thought, 'Arnold must have a hobby', and it went on from there. Arnold Layne just happens to dig dressing up in women's clothing. A lot of people do - so let's face up to reality. About the only other lyric anybody could object to, is the bit about, 'It takes two to know' and there's nothing 'smutty' about that! But then if more people like them dislike us, more people like the underground lot are going to dig us, so we hope they'll cancel each other out."

Syd was referring to the shock and horror exhibited by the more prudish members of British society such as the pirate radio station Radio London who regarded it as "too smutty" for them to play. Presumably they had not been paid enough payola by EMI to like it. It is not as if this sort of thing was new to British pop music; in March 1966 The Kinks had a chart hit with 'Dedicated Follower Of Fashion' with a very camp reading of the line "and when he pulls his frilly nylon panties right up tight." Maybe he got them from Arnold.

The puritanical outrage did seem to surprise the band who held varying opinions, ranging from Syd's dismissal of it as something business men did - "It's only a business-like commercial insult anyway. It doesn't affect us personally" - to Rick's view that it was a paranoid fear of the underground: "I think the record was banned not because of the lyrics, because there's nothing there you can really object to - but because they're against us as a group and against what we stand for.'

Roger took a more moderate view: "Let's face it, the pirate stations play records that are much more 'smutty' than 'Arnold Layne' will ever be. In fact, it's only Radio London that has banned the record. The BBC and everybody else plays it. I think it's just different policies - not anything against us."

Though not a top ten hit, 'Arnold Layne' reached number 20 in the *Record Mirror* chart before dropping out again. On March 10, the group played UFO and premiered a promo film* they made for the single which was in the shops that day. By then the Floyd were already at Abbey Road recording their first album because, unusually, they had been signed on an album deal, not to solely make singles. Boyd's replacement turned out to be Norman 'Hurricane' Smith, whose qualification was that he had engineered innumerable Beatles sessions under the stewardship of George Martin. EMI wanted him to graduate to production, and presumably thought that he could hone his skills on this new malleable group, seeing him as performing the sort of role George Martin had with the Beatles: producer, musical adviser and arranger. After unsuccessfully attempting to reproduce the performance and sound quality of 'Arnold Layne' at Abbey Road, EMI reluctantly went ahead and released Joe's Sound Techniques' masters.

Having got the business of the single out of the way, work on the Floyd's first album commenced on February 21, with an all-night session to record 'Matilda Mother', Syd's beautiful evocation of a mother reading a bedtime story to her child. There was a distinctive Abbey Road sound in the mid Sixties and Norman 'Hurricane' Smith had learned all the EMI recording tricks such as double tracking combined with a soupcon

*EMI tried to keep everything in-house; they even built their own mixing desks.

*Boyd's ears were attuned to the times: the day after recording 'Arnold Layne' he recorded the Purple Gang's 'Granny Takes A Trip' at Sound Techniques which became another UFO favourite and would have gone further had not Peter 'Lucifer,' Walker, their leader, disbanded the group in order to train to be initiated as a Warlock.

*The surreal B&W clip featured the group larking about on a beach on a grey day with a tailoring dummy.

of echo on certain vocals and he was able to give these a touch of phasing. The group recorded in Studio 3, using a little four-track that, in addition to all the wonderful gadgetry of the time – now found in museums only – had a memorable feature that summed up the recording ethos at EMI: a knob that said 'pop' and 'classical'. The former setting gave a more subtle gradation to the faders whereas the latter was more abrupt, to cater to the cruder nature of the music. Like all the decks at EMI, the company had built it themselves.

Though the Floyd had engaged in some rather unseemly leaping about outside EMI's Manchester Square headquarters for the benefit of photographers on the occasion of their signing, they did not go along with most attempts to market them. Roger told *Disc and Music Echo*: "I lie and am rather aggressive" and told the clearly puzzled reporter: "We give the public what they can see for themselves – we don't want to manufacture an image. We don't want to be involved in some publicity build-up."

THE PIPER AT THE GATES OF DAWN

With the exception of Roger Waters' 'Take Up Thy Stethoscope And Walk', the Pink Floyd's first album, *The Piper At The Gates Of Dawn* is made up of Syd Barrett songs and some group instrumentals. In the six months from the summer of 1966 Syd had gone through a period of exceptional creativity at Earlham Street. He painted, played music, read voraciously, listened widely, smoked a lot of pot and took long voyages in his own head; this was the time he first began to take a large amount of acid. It was also the time during which he wrote virtually everything upon which his reputation as a songwriter is based.

It is a peculiarly English version of psychedelia that makes up *The Piper At The Gates Of Dawn*, the title of which, appropriately is taken from chapter seven of Kenneth Grahame's children's book *The Wind In The Willows*. Much of English psychedelia refers back to childhood, a period of innocence and purity populated by gnomes and fairies, elves and dwarves. Peter Jenner thought that the last time Syd felt really happy was before his father's death, so childhood became a refuge from the pressures of the modern world, a way of returning to the carefree pleasures of playing in Grantchester Meadows with his sister Rosemary, to lie down and watch the river flow by, listening to the distant bells (the subject of 'Flaming').

In this chapter of *Wind In The Willows* Rat and Mole encounter Pan, the mischievous Dionysian half-man, half-goat, much loved by Picasso, who was very much in the news in the late Fifties and early Sixties. The huge Tate Gallery show in July 1960 was almost certainly attended by Syd and throughout the Sixties, reproductions of Picasso's Pan figures were to be found on middle-class living room walls and in the newly published Sunday newspaper colour supplements.

Pan is used by Grahame to convey rather profound spiritual concepts about elemental forces and the afterlife to his young readers. Cliff Jones in his perceptive essay 'Wish You Were Here' makes the point that when Rat and Mole meet Pan "the god of flocks, woods and fields", they encounter him as "a golden, dream-like vision". This intrigued Syd, who took the episode as the central beam of his writing for the album. And not just that, Syd would often inform friends of how he too had met Pan and been instilled with "the spirit of the forest." Andrew King said, "He thought Pan had given him insight and understanding into the way nature works." This then is the origin of the fairy-tale imagery, the mice and gnomes that permeate the album.

Syd absorbed information from everywhere, some of which he appropriated straight, some of which came out in undigested form, for instance, when the Floyd first performed 'Matilda Mother', Syd blatantly lifted lyrics from Hilaire Belloc's *Cautionary Tales*. In order to record them, Andrew King had to approach the Hilaire Belloc estate for permission for their use but was refused.* Although the lyrics were rewritten the title still reflected Belloc's 'Matilda, Who Told Lies And Was Burned To Death.'

Syd: 'I do tend to take lines from other things, lines I like, and then write around them but I don't consciously relate to painting. It's just writing good songs that matters, really.' The lyrics were of great importance to him: 'I think it's good if a song has more than one meaning. Maybe that kind of song can reach far more people, that's nice. On the other hand, I like songs that are simple. I liked 'Arnold Layne' because to me it was a very clear song.'

Barrett's approach to songwriting owes much to the abstract expressionist painting that still dominated the art world at that time; it is an immediate response to

*Because Belloc died in 1872 it's hard to see how they could have still been in copyright.

*In this case Syd used the lyrics word-for-word, changing only one word: 'merry' became 'midnight.'

*Even now bikes far outnumber cars in Cambridge and are the most common mode of transport.

**Above: From
the Piper At
The Gates Of
Dawn album
sleeve shoot.**

surroundings. The lyrics are often descriptions of what he was wearing or what was happening at that very moment; word sketches in the Jack Kerouac sense of literally making word pictures of what was going on around him or in his head.

The second recording session for *Piper*, on February 27, began with 'Chapter 24'; another case of Syd copping his lyrics from another source. In this case it was the notes to chapter 24 of the *I-Ching* or *Book Of Changes*, the Chinese oracle text that he first encountered in Cambridge on Seamus O'Connell's mother's bookshelves. Chapter 24 is the Fû hexagram or 'Yoni Of Fire' (K'un, the receptive earth, Chen, the arousing thunder, as the Wilhelm edition rather prudishly translates it) and Syd lifted the words to 'Chapter 24' from it almost verbatim: "All movements are accomplished in six stages and the seventh brings return ... Therefore seven is the number of the young light, and it arises when six, the number of great darkness, is increased by one." This is taken from the Richard Wilhelm translation that Syd owned at the time.

The *I-Ching* was popular hippie reading matter, and many people would not go out without first throwing the *I-Ching* to see what it advised. Syd: "That ['Chapter 24'] was from *I Ching*, there was someone around who was very into that, most of the words came straight off that."

While running the Indica Bookshop I remember Syd coming in and buying a copy of the Wilhelm edition, though I think it was a present for the girl he had with him. He was possibly inspired to rework the *I-Ching* after hearing that John Lennon had used Timothy Leary's version of the *Tibetan Book Of The Dead* as inspiration for the lyrics to 'Tomorrow Never Knows'; "Turn off your mind, relax, and drift downstream" being from Leary's introduction. Syd appropriated lyrics from wherever he found them: 'Golden Hair', on Barrett's first solo album *The Madcap Laughs*, was an untitled early James Joyce poem, the fifth in the volume *Chamber Music* published in 1907, that Syd set to music while still in his teens.*

As word sketches of memories or descriptions of what was happening to him at that moment, Syd's lyrics on the album constitute fragments of autobiography. It is not surprising, then, that there is a preoccupation with childhood and frequent images of Cambridge. 'Bike', one of Barrett's classic songs, is like one of Duchamp's 'found objects': only Syd would take such a commonplace object and write a song about it.* Though Syd himself wore a cloak onstage in the early days, I don't recall it being black and red and I would like to think that the cloak referred to in the second verse is in fact an academic gown. It is only in Oxford and Cambridge that it is common to see people on the streets wearing academic gowns, or cloaks, often in red and black as described, and it is just the sort of thing that Syd might have got his hands on. Perhaps the line refers to both sorts.

'Astronomy Domine' was a recollection of Syd's aforementioned acid trip when a plum and an orange became Venus and Jupiter. Barrett was aided in his astronomical whimsy by a copy of the small *Times Atlas Of The Planets* and Peter Jenner who helped him in writing those parts. It is Jenner's garbled planetary recitations that open the track, and therefore the album.

'Lucifer Sam', originally called 'Percy The Ratcatcher', is a word sketch of a cat in the room, Syd's fey English voice making the song strangely effective as well as it being a typical piece of Swinging London pop of the period. Syd: "It didn't mean much to me at the time, but then three or four months later it came to mean a lot." 'Scarecrow' sounds like a reference to the scarecrow in Derek McCulloch (Uncle Mac)'s BBC Radio *Children's Hour* programmes of the late Forties and early Fifties. 'Flaming' and 'The Gnome' have their origins in Cambridge: buttercups and dandelions on Grantchester Meadows in 'Flaming', and the winding River Cam in 'The Gnome'.

For this writer the inclusion on *Piper* of the adventures of a gnome called Grimble Gromble was most unfortunate. All one can say in its defence is that novelty tracks seemed to be an aberration shared by many British groups at the time: from Cream's 'Mother's Lament' (on *Disraeli Gears*) to Tomorrow's 'Three Jolly Little Dwarfs'. 'The Gnome' does of course fall into the fairy-tale, nursery rhyme category; an escape to the past obviously inspired by J. R. R. Tolkien. Syd: "Fairy tales are nice... I think a lot of it has to do with living in Cambridge, with nature and everything. It's so clean, and I still drive back a lot. Maybe if I'd stayed at college, I would have become a teacher. Leaving school and suddenly being without that structure around you and nothing to relate to... maybe that's a part of it, too."

The band were quite pleased with their efforts and enjoyed making the album. Syd: "That was very difficult in some ways, getting used to the studios and everything. But

THE PINK FLOYD EXPERIENCE

it was fun, we freaked about a lot. I was working very hard then." One of the highlights was the fact that three of the Beatles, who were making *Sgt. Pepper* in Studio 2 next door, stopped by to visit and give the Pink Floyd encouragement. I was watching the Beatles session at the time and ran into one of the Floyd's entourage in the canteen who told me they were there. I had previously taken Paul McCartney to see the group at UFO so I suggested he might stop by and say hello to his fellow EMI recording artists. Paul gathered up Ringo and George and we all went into Studio 3.

Roger Waters: "At about 5:30 in the afternoon Ringo, Paul and George came into our studio and we all stood rooted to the spot, excited by it all. Of course UFO was really a big scene by then." To me the Floyd seemed very nervous, not of the Beatles, but of the actual recording set-up and I remember Roger trying to shout to Norman Smith through the thick soundproof glass control room window instead of using the open microphone provided for that purpose. These were their early days in the studio environment and they had not got the hang of it yet; however it did not take long for them to develop such technical mastery that the studio itself became their instrument. I understand that Paul, at least, often popped his head in to see how they were doing whenever Beatles and Floyd sessions overlapped. In the February 15, 1967 issue of *Cherwell*, Oxford University's weekly paper, one of the Floyd, probably Syd, said "At the moment Paul McCartney is probably the single greatest influence on us." McCartney returned the compliment by declaring to the music press that the Floyd's album was "a knockout."

The Piper At The Gates Of Dawn was released on August 5, 1967 and reached number 6 in the UK album charts, staying seven weeks in the Top 20. Though the album received a good reception, there was a general consensus among the band's admirers that the album was a poor second to their live performance. It is an interesting album because it shows that despite their confusion when Syd left the band, many of their post-Barrett concerns were already in place with the large scale sound environments and controlled atmospheres that they later made entirely their own. 'Bike', with its prescient coda of clockwork and other sound effects, even prefigured *Dark Side Of The Moon*. The arrangement and the extended improvisation on 'Interstellar Overdrive' was a collaborative effort by all four members of the band and, more than anything, pointed the direction in which they were to go.

Nick: "Our album shows parts of the Pink Floyd that haven't been heard yet."

Roger: "There's a part we haven't even heard yet."

Nick: "It's bringing into flower many of the fruits that remained dormant for so long."

Syd: "It all comes straight out of our heads and it's not too far out to understand. If we play well on stage I think most people understand that what we play isn't just a noise. Most audiences respond to a good set."

GAMES FOR MAY

Before the album was released, the Pink Floyd had another go at the pop charts – this time with 'See Emily Play.' The song was specially written for another classical event, called 'Games For May', promoted by Christopher Hunt on May 12, 1967 at the Queen Elizabeth Hall on the South Bank.

The advertisement read more like a notice for UFO than for a classical music venue:

SPACE-AGE RELAXATION FOR THE CLIMAX OF SPRING – ELECTRONIC COMPOSITIONS, COLOUR AND IMAGE PROJECTIONS, GIRLS AND THE PINK FLOYD.

Hunt released a press release saying: "The Floyd intend this concert to be a musical and visual exploration – not only for themselves, but for the audience too. New material has been written and will be given for the first time, including some specially prepared four-way stereo tapes. Visually the lights-men of the group have prepared an entirely new, bigger-than-ever-before show. Sadly we are not allowed to throw lighting effects as planned onto the external surfaces of the hall, nor even in the foyer. But inside should be enough!"

Roger Waters was responsible for the opening music, which sounded like the dawn chorus but which he actually created on tape. He told Chris Salewicz: 'I was working in this dank, dingy basement off the Harrow Road, with an old Ferrograph. I remember sitting there recording edge tones off cymbals for the performance – later that became the beginning of 'A Saucerful Of Secrets'. In those days you could get away with stuff like chasing clockwork toy cars around the stage with a microphone. For 'Games For

May' I also made 'bird' noises recorded on the old Ferrograph at half-speed, to be played in the theatre's foyer as the audience was coming in. I was always interested in the possibilities of rock 'n' roll, how to fill the space between the audience and the idea with more than just guitars and vocals." The band had to give up a week's work to rehearse the songs however, apart from the lights and quadrophonic sound mix, they did not actually plan the performance until the day itself. They rehearsed on stage the morning of the show to try and work up their act but, by the time the audience began filing in to the QEH, they still had not figured out exactly what to do.

Roger: "We just took a lot props onstage with us and improvised. Quite a bit of what we did went down quite well, but a lot of it got completely lost. We worked out a fantastic stereophonic sound system whereby the sounds travelled around the hall in a sort of circle, giving the audience an eerie effect of being absolutely surrounded by the music – and of course we tried to help the effect by the use of our lighting. Unfortunately it only worked for people sitting in the front of the hall – still, this was the first time we'd tried it, and like a lot of other ideas we used for the first time at this concert, they should be improved by the time we do our next one. Also, we thought we'd be able to use the props and work our act out as we went along – but we found this extremely difficult. I think it's important to know what you're going to do – to a certain extent anyway, I always like to be in control of a situation. Another thing we found out from giving that concert was that our ideas were far more advanced than our musical capabilities – at that time anyway... we made a lot of mistakes at that concert, but it was the first of its kind and we, personally learnt a lot from it."

EMI helped out by erecting huge speakers at the back of the hall to complement the Floyd's own PA onstage and lending their expertise to help create the first quadraphonic PA system ever built in Britain (perhaps anywhere). This was controlled by a primitive joystick apparatus that could place both pre-recorded tapes and the instruments at any point within the circle made by the speakers. The light show was beefed up by the addition of 35mm film projections as well as the usual pulsating oil slides turning the hall into a cross between UFO and Santa's grotto.

The show opened with Roger's prerecorded tapes and the original set-list ran as follows: 'Matilda Mother', 'Flaming', 'Scarecrow', 'Games For May' (aka 'See Emily Play'), 'Bicycle' (aka 'Bike'), 'Arnold Layne', 'Candy And A Currant Bun', 'Pow R Toc H', and 'Interstellar Overdrive'. The concert ended with a tape by Rick Wright called 'Bubbles' followed by a tape by Syd, and 'Lucifer Sam' which was presumably the encore.

'Bubbles' was accompanied by the release of millions of actual bubbles and a Floyd roadie dressed as an admiral of the fleet who came onstage carrying armloads of daffodils and threw them to the audience. Unfortunately, to the dismay of the hall's management, when the bubbles burst they left a ring on the leather seats – thousands of them – and the daffodils were not all skillfully caught by the audience: some were trampled into the carpet. As a result, the Floyd were banned from ever appearing again at the Queen Elizabeth Hall.

Roger: "It seems we contravened a regulation. We were told that people might have slipped on the flowers we threw into the audience." This was the height of flower power and the majority of the audience were in their finest hippie gear: frills, tatty lace and velvet, see through chiffon and crushed velvet as well as face paint, refractive third-eye lenses and extraordinary eye makeup were the norm. The *Financial Times* reported, "The audience which filled the hall was beautiful, if strangely subdued, and to enjoy them was alone worth the price of the ticket. But when you add the irrepressible Pink Floyd and a free authentic daffodil to take home, your cup of experience overflows."

Roger reported: "Someone I know was sitting next to two old ladies who sat there still and silent until the interval. Then one turned to her friend and said, 'They're very good, aren't they?'"

The Games For May concert can be seen as the precursor of Pink Floyd's stadium shows, and ultimately of *The Wall*. The use of quad sound was an enormous breakthrough and is further proof that the Floyd's career trajectory, rather than breaking into pre and post Barrett phases, was pretty well established from day one. From then on the Floyd used a quadraphonic sound mix wherever possible, developing their famed 'Azimuth Co-ordinator' or quadraphonic pan pot to do the job – the original one from Queen Elizabeth Hall having been stolen.

SEE EMILY PLAY

'Games For May' was identified by everyone as an obvious hit single, even Norman Smith who had great trouble in dealing with Syd because he would never play a song the same way twice.

"I saw that as a single straight away," Smith told Nicky Horne, "and obviously one was looking for a follow-up to 'Arnold Layne' – I was at any rate, on behalf of the record company. It was a pretty difficult job with Syd because I think Syd... used lyrics with sort of musical phrasing, and it was a statement being made at a given time, that meant that if you came back five minutes later to do another take you probably wouldn't get the same performance, and I think if I remember rightly we went through quite a few of Syd's songs and then they played me a few, and it's very difficult to pick out which I liked and which I didn't like, so we'd come back and maybe try these songs again and these were different versions so it made it even more difficult. So the early days were quite difficult really but as a sort of very slow, unwinding process."

Although the group was in the middle of a vocal overdubbing session for 'Bike' they decamped to Sound Techniques to record 'See Emily Play'. There was either no time available at Abbey Road – which is unlikely – or they preferred the sound at Sound Techniques – which is probably the case. For whatever reason John Wood was amused to see mighty EMI's studios rejected in favour of Sound Techniques when the band wanted to get a good sound. Exact recording dates are not available but 'Emily' was recorded either on May 18 or that weekend, on the 20 and 21. The Floyd took their EMI tape op, Jeff Jarrett with them which suggests that it was entirely a matter of sound that determined their choice.

There are varying reports of the sessions. David Gilmour, for instance, was shocked to see how out of it Syd was. David was living and working in Paris with his band Flowers when they had all of their microphones stolen. He came to London to replace them as you could buy secondhand Shures on Lisle Street in Soho for £7 when the same model in Paris was £35 new. Gilmour told Mark Paytress: "I don't know at quite what point Syd started to go very strange, but I know I came back from France and I called Syd up while I was there and he said, 'Why don't you come down?' They were recording and he told me to come down to the studio. And I went down there and he didn't even recognise me."

Gilmour had not seen Barrett in more than a year and the change was dramatic. Syd just stared back. 'He was a different person from the one I'd last seen in October. I'd done plenty of acid and dope – often with Syd – and that was different from how he had become."

To the members of the band the change had, of course, been gradual and perhaps they did not see to what extent Syd's personality had changed. This was made especially difficult because the group had a working relationship as well as an old friendship. This particular day is a good case in point as musically it was by all accounts a brilliant session; Syd was right on form, the vocals sounded good, and the group had themselves a hit single. No one had any experience of mental illness and there were as yet few examples of acid casualties. Everyone just hoped for the best as there was little else they could do.

The lyrics for 'See Emily Play' had nestled in Syd's ring binder for some time. All that was required was to change the name from 'Games For May' to 'See Emily Play'. The words dated back to the London Free School period and were inspired by the Honourable Emily Tacita Young, 15-year-old daughter of Labour MP Wayland Young, Lord Kennet. Emily and her best friend Anjelica Houston attended Holland Park Comprehensive and were regulars at the London Free School's basement and at the All Saints' Hall dances where she was known as 'Far Out Em'. (Later, at UFO, she was called 'the psychedelic schoolgirl'). Peter Jenner lived in Notting Hill and after one LFS gig she went back to his house with Syd and spent hours smoking pot and talking. The next day Syd wrote 'See Emily Play' about her youthful naivety.

The music was composed just before the concert in May at a flat owned by Andrew King's parents in Richmond Hill, which he shared with Rick Wright. Rick, being the musical one of the group, had set up a primitive demo studio in the living room with a number of tape recorders and other equipment. The studio was used by the Floyd to work out ideas and rehearse, much to the dismay of Andrew's wealthy neighbours. Syd and Lynsey moved into the spare room and King remembers Syd finding the lyrics and composing the 'Games for May' line because they needed something special for the concert. The Richmond interlude appears to have been a good period for Syd and Lynsey living in pleasant surroundings with the band hovering on the brink of fame.

King told David Parker: "It was a very nice room... looked right across the Thames Valley. The Bentley was parked on the pavement outside. The Pink Floyd Bentley. Yes, we used to go to gigs in the Bentley." He neglected to say that it wasn't a new one, nonetheless, it was classier than the Beatles Austin Princess. 'See Emily Play' was released on June 16, 1967 at the height of the Summer of Love, and reached number six in the charts. The Pink Floyd had a Top 10 single.

It must have been excruciatingly difficult for the band to find themselves on the verge of pop success, and yet to find that Syd, who after all wrote and sang the song, was simultaneously sabotaging it all. Part of him delighted in the fame, the money, pop-star clothes, but there was another Syd, the bohemian, who rejected the lot of it. The more pressure there was on him, the more he vacillated between the two polar positions.

Roger Waters: "When he was still in the band in the later stages, we got to the point where anyone of us was likely to tear his throat out at any minute because he was so impossible... When 'Emily' was a hit and we were third for three weeks, we did *Top Of The Pops*, and the third week we did it he didn't want to know. He got down there in an incredible state and said he wasn't gonna do it. We finally discovered the reason was that John Lennon didn't have to do *Top Of The Pops* so he didn't."

At first Syd seemed pleased to be on *Top Of The Pops*, miming his song and playing the role of pop star. In fact Syd once stated that the Pink Floyd were pop stars first and musicians second, and totally agreed that the lavish pop lifestyle was what he wanted, but in this, as in many other things, his attitude was schizophrenic, and the 'underground' part of him rejected all that false glamour. *TOTP* only featured acts that were in the charts, so some bands found themselves on it for many weeks in a row. On the second week, Syd arrived in his full Kings Road finery then changed into shabby student clothes for the programme but by the third week, where a really good showing might have pushed them to number two (Procul Harum's 'A Whiter Shade Of Pale' was firmly ensconced at number one), Syd refused to appear at all. This was a time when a chart single was a very strong determining factor in the price a band could charge for a live show and a Top 10 single could double your fee, so everyone was understandably keen to do a good job. Except Syd, who, that day, was a Keith Rowe musical purist.

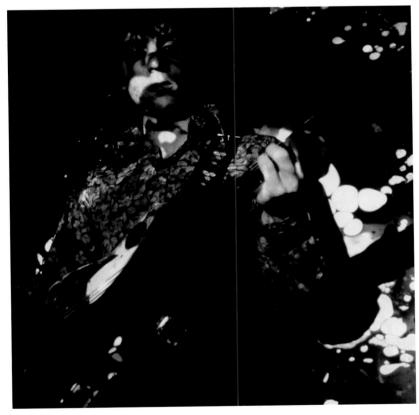

CHAPTER EIGHT
ON THE ROAD

CHAPTER EIGHT
ON THE ROAD

The greatest fans of *International Times* were the police who poured over every word. They raided a 60-year old potter in Cornwall because he'd innocently advertised a pug mill for sale in *IT*'s classifieds. A pug mill is used to prepare clay to make pots but to them, of course, it had to be something to do with drugs.

On March 9, 1967, the police made a determined effort to close down the paper. In a heavy-handed action in every way the same as the behaviour of the Stasi or some South American dictatorship a gang of them arrived with an obscene publications warrant and took away every scrap of paper in the office including all back issues, the telephone books, invoices, staff members' address books and even uncashed cheques. They illegally body searched the staff members and carefully examined the ashtrays for pornography. They then threw everything in the back of a three ton truck and took it away. After three and a half months they returned it all in complete disarray, without bringing any charges.

This would have closed down any normal business, which had been their intention, but *IT* was not primarily a business. The police had intimated that if we dared to print another issue, they might return and seize that too, so while we took legal advice, the contents of the next issue were published by being read aloud at the UFO Club. The original warrant was issued because someone, thought to be the right-wing Christian MP Sir Cyril Black, had objected to American comedian Dick Gregory's use of the word 'motherfucker' in an interview. However the friendly MP Tom Driberg told me that the raid was ordered by Lord Goodman, Harold Wilson's private lawyer who objected to his godson's involvement in the paper.

Even before the paper was busted, Hoppy and several other *IT* staff had been organising a monster benefit event to shore up the paper's ailing finances. With the prospect of an expensive obscenity case in the offing, planning for what became the 14-Hour Technicolour Dream was suddenly intensified. Michael McInnerney designed a beautiful silk-screened rainbow poster for the event – no two alike – and UFO poster designers Michael English and Nigel Waymouth, made a huge black and white poster for major ad sites. In one publicity stunt four girls walked down Portobello Road, each with a letter painted on the back of their white T-shirts: Sue had 'F'; Zoe had 'U', Kitty was 'C' and Pru was 'K. The police reacted at once and asked the girls to "arrange themselves in less provocative groups," which had the desired effect of getting the story into the newspapers. A *Melody Maker* ad for the 14-Hour Technicolor Dream read: "a giant benefit against fuzz action". One ad promised "Kaleidoscopic colour, beautiful people" and revealed that the event would be followed by a "free be-in on Sunday".

At dusk on Saturday, April 29 rockets burst over the London skyline like a bat signal telling the freaks to come out. The 14-Hour Technicolor Dream benefit was held at

Alexandra Palace, a huge Victorian glass and steel pleasure palace, even bigger than the Royal Albert Hall, set in the middle of a park in north London. The city's first television transmitter was mounted on one of its towers because of its prominent position. In the early Sixties it was used as the venue for all night jazz raves, which is probably why Hoppy thought of it.

Among the people who had donated their time and talents to the benefit were the Pink Floyd, Alexis Korner, the Pretty Things, the Purple Gang, Champion Jack Dupree, Graham Bond, Yoko Ono, Savoy Brown, the Flies, Ginger Johnson's Drummers, the Crazy World of Arthur Brown, Soft Machine, the Creation, Denny Laine, Sam Gopal, Giant Sun Trolley, Social Deviants, the Block, the Cat, Charlie Brown's Clowns, Christopher Logue, Derek Brimstone, Dave Russell, Glo Macari and the Big Three, Gary Farr, the Interference, Jacobs Ladder Construction Company, Lincoln Folk Group, the Move, Mike Horovitz, 117, Poison Bellows, Pete Townshend, Robert Randall, Suzy Creamcheese, Mick and Pete, The Stalkers, Utterly Incredible Too Long Ago To Remember, Sometimes Shouting At People, Barry Fantoni, Noel Murphy and various others.

Many of these were poets, performance artists or dance groups, but the only way to ensure they all got to perform was to erect two stages, one each end of the giant hall. Many people, with chemically enhanced hearing, liked to stand sideways in the strange neutral zone midway between the stages where both could be heard at equal volume in glorious stereo.

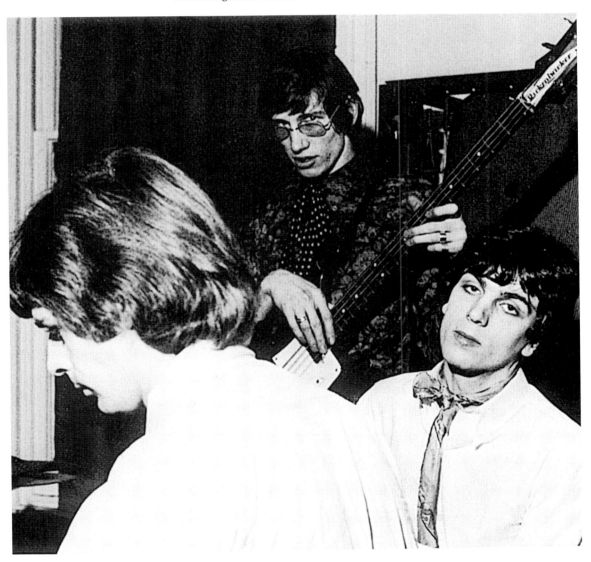

Huge white sheets had been hung on either side of the galleries for the light shows and a light board, like the one on Times Square, spelled out moving messages the way the news was displayed on the *Times* building. Hoppy and the UFO staff controlled the lights and sound from a huge gantry in the centre of the hall. There was a fairground helter skelter offering free rides to anyone prepared to climb the steps to the top and a fibreglass igloo where Hoppy's girlfriend, Suzy Creamcheese, handed out dried banana skins for people to smoke – that month's harmless hippie fad. David Medalla and the Exploding Galaxy danced, poets read their texts, folk-singers strummed, people cast the I-Ching and doled out tarot cards, Yoko Ono demonstrated her Cut Piece where a model's clothing was cut off by members of the audience using a pair of scissors. John Lennon and Indica Gallery owner John Dunbar saw footage of the event on the BBC-TV nine o'clock news, jumped in Lennon's Rolls-Royce and arrived high on acid.

As was usual at UFO, much of the entertainment was of the do-it-yourself variety; the audience *was* the event and many people made long lasting friendships there. Desmond from Notting Hill, for instance, stationed himself at the entrance and greeted people on arrival and received more than 40 visitors in the weeks afterwards as a result of his conversations with strangers at the door.

A few skinheads who'd arrived hoping to cause a spot of aggro were love-bombed by a group of girls in lace and velvet dresses and were soon seen skipping hand in hand with the girls out of their heads on acid. The only hitch in the proceedings came at midnight when people started climbing up the scaffolding. Naturally, the event was not insured so the music had to be stopped in order to get them down. The Ally Pally was like an enormously enlarged UFO club and felt very familiar and comfortable. This was partly due to the line-up of UFO regulars: Arthur Brown, who gave an inspired performance, doing his very best to transform himself into the God of Hellfire; the Soft Machine dressed up specially for the occasion: Daevid Allen in a miner's helmet, Mike Ratledge in his Dr. Strange cape, Kevin Ayers with rouged cheeks and wide brimmed hat, and Robert Wyatt with a short-back and sides.

Daevid Allen: "As I recall, the Floyd played at Alexandra Palace at four in the morning. It must have been one of the greatest gigs they ever did, and Syd played with a slide and it completely blew my mind, because I was hearing echoes of all the music I'd ever heard with bits of Bartok and God-knows-what." That would seem to dispel reports that Syd was so out of it that he just stared at the audience.

The Pink Floyd arrived around 3.30 am having played a gig in Holland that evening and returned on the ferry. They were tired and exhausted and both Syd and Peter Jenner were tripping. Peter Jenner: "I dropped a tab on the way to the gig and it started coming on as we were being directed in. I was having to steer the van through something very tiny and lots of people were wondering about all absolutely out of their crust. There were people climbing over scaffolding and it was an extraordinary building with all the glass in the Alley Pally... as the light came up, because it was the summer [sic] ... it was a wonderful, really a psychedelic experience. The whole world was there and every band was playing and it was a magical occasion."

The Floyd had specifically asked to go on at dawn and as the Floyd's roadies began setting up on the 10 foot high stage, the crowd pushed forwards. There were about 10,000 people there but the hall held many times that number and most of the space was half empty, like an airport with people wandering about. I can do little better than reprint my own description of the event which, though not contemporary, was written decades closer to the time than now.

"The band went on just as the first fingers of dawn entered through the enormous rose windows, the throbbing bass line of 'Interstellar Overdrive' galvanising the crowd. Their music was eerie, solemn and calming. After a whole night of frolicking and festivities and too much acid came the celebration of the dawn. Throughout the hall people held hands with their neighbours. The Floyd were weary and probably did not play so well but at that moment they were superb. They gave voice to the feelings of the crowd. Syd's eyes blazed as his notes soared up into the strengthening light and the dawn was reflected in his famous mirror-disc Esquire, the light dancing in the crowd. Then came the rebirth of energy, another day, and with the sun a burst of dancing and enthusiasm."

As people left, Hoppy stood at the entrance shaking hands with everyone as if it had been a private dinner party. At the Sunday Be-In, held in the park surrounding Ally Pally, some hippies had rolled a 10 foot long joint from photo studio backdrop paper, filled with flowers and leaves, and were running around on the grass with it. The skinheads, having now come down again, stole it from them and spent a happy hour reasserting their identities by kicking the monster to pieces.

101 CROMWELL ROAD

After Richmond, Syd and Lynsey, accompanied by Mad Sue and Mad Jock from Earlham Street, moved to one of the many bedrooms in the top maisonette at 101 Cromwell Road. It was a big mistake. Floyd roadie John Marsh described Syd's room-mates to Jonathon Green, one of "...whom was a psychotic kind of character called Scotty. He was one of the original 'put acid-in-the-reservoir, change the face-of-the-world' acid missionaries. He was also a desperately twisted freak and really malevolent crazy."

According to Marsh, Scottie's thing was spiking everything with acid and people knew that if you visited Syd you should never have a cup of tea or a glass of water unless you got it yourself from the tap. There was acid in the morning coffee, acid in everything. They even gave it to the cat. Everyone knew what was happening but no one had the intelligence to move Syd out so consequently, he got worse and worse.

John Marsh: "Poor Syd was really in the poo... but nobody had the courage or wished to be thought uncool enough to dig Syd out of this situation... and he was going further and further down the tubes." Eventually his old Cambridge friends Storm and Po – Storm Thorgerson and Aubrey Powell from designers Hipgnosis – came and rescued him and took he and Lynsey to live at their flat in Egerton Court, a huge, soulless, eight-story red brick Thirties mansion block on the south side of Old Brompton Road at Cromwell Place, across from the South Kensington underground station. Nigel and Jenny Lesmoire-Gordon had already moved there as 101 was going to be demolished to make way for the expansion of the West London Air Terminal, in fact their ground floor flat was already boarded up, prior to demolition.

EGERTON COURT

Despite the building's grim exterior, Egerton Court was one of the many 'cool pads' on the Sixties scene, somewhere that Pete Townshend or Mick Jagger and Marianne Faithfull felt they could drop by and be assured to find a pleasant scene in progress and where no one would hassle them. Unfortunately Syd's grasp of reality was now deteriorating rapidly. Though Syd was never violent towards the members of the band, stories abounded of his mistreatment of women. Although Lynsey has always refused to confirm that he was violent towards her, many people claimed to have witnessed him hit her and three of the residents of Egerton Court confirm that he once smashed his guitar over her head. Po says, 'I remember pulling Syd off her.'

Syd's sister Rosemary agreed that he always had a violent side and never had much self control. He was always able to get away with anything he wanted at home and he attracted girls who were prepared to be dominated by him. Whether he really kept her locked in her room for three days and fed her biscuits under the door is another matter, one would hope that the other residents would have intervened if this was really the case. One story that circulated at UFO was that one night she stayed overnight in a hostel and he became convinced that she was sleeping with someone else and set off the building's fire alarm. Syd apparently stood across the road watching to see if she came out with anyone as the confused residents stumbled in to the street in their nightclothes.

HARD TIMES IN THE COUNTRY

The Pink Floyd was generally well received by the London audience who appreciated their experimentation. Even if the results did not come off that well, the group was applauded for the effort. It was not the same in the provinces. Here the audiences only knew them as a chart act and beyond that they wanted to be able to dance.

Roger: "We started touring about England disastrously... It wasn't a real tour, it was all ballrooms, Top Rank sort of thing, and the audiences really hated us. Even at that time we were pretty bolshy. We thought, 'All right, 'See Emily Play' was a nice single, but not the sort of thing a chap wants to play.' So we wouldn't play it, and they threw beer cans and coins at us. We cleared more halls than you've had hot dinners."

Nick Mason: "During that period we were working at Top Rank circuits, and they *hated* it. I *hated* it. We could clear halls so fast it wasn't true. I mean they were outraged by what came round on the revolving stage and they lost very little time in trying to make this clear, and the only place we played with any sort of success, or real interest, was UFO, and the various underground-in-inverted commas clubs and occasions. There'd be this revolving stage and the audience out in front who were hoping to hear 'Arnold Layne' and 'See Emily Play' and a host of other hits, which we couldn't of course play. We had a repertoire of *strange* things like 'Interstellar Overdrive' to carry us through that whole set. I just remember the stages going round and this audience just appalled by what they saw in front of them. And, I mean, the whole thing was fantastic anyway, because... what was then considered to be our audience of course could never get into these places because you had to have a tie to get in, and there was the whole business of they wouldn't let us drink at the bar because we hadn't got collars and ties, and various outrages that used to drive us all mad."

Sometimes touring the provinces could be physically threatening. When the Floyd played the California Ballroom in Dunstable, Bedfordshire, on February 18, the local punters poured pints of beer onto them from the balcony which could have caused a fatal electric shock had it wetted the wrong piece of equipment whereas at East Dereham broken beer mugs were thrown at the bass drum.

Roger: "The worst thing that ever happened to me was at the Feathers Club in Ealing, which was a penny, which made a bloody great cut in the middle of my forehead. I bled quite a lot. And I stood right at the front of the stage to see if I could see him throw one. I was glowering in a real rage, and I was gonna leap out into the audience and get him. Happily there was one freak who turned up who liked us, so the audience spent the whole evening beating the shit out of him."

Roger Waters told Chris Welch the same thing in August: "We're being frustrated at the moment by the fact that to stay alive we have to play lots and lots of places and venues that are not really suitable. We've got a name of sorts now among the public so everybody comes to have a look at us, and we get full houses. But the atmosphere in these places is very stale. There is no feeling of occasion. There is no nastiness about it, but we don't get rebooked on the club or ballroom circuit. What I'm trying to say is that the sort of thing we are trying to do doesn't fit into the sort of environment we are playing in. The supporting bands play 'Midnight Hour' and the records are all soul, then we come on.'

Roger said that it was virtually impossible to reproduce the sort of record they make on stage, particularly the special effects on their album. "We still do 'Arnold Layne' and struggle through 'Emily' occasionally. We don't think it's dishonest because we can't play live what we play on records. It's a perfectly ok scene. Can you imagine somebody trying to play 'A Day In The Life'? Yet that's one of the greatest tracks ever made. A lot of stuff on our LP is completely impossible to do live."

Clearly it was this disparity between the stage and the studio that led to the creation of the Floyd spectacle, a way of giving something utterly different from their recorded music to the audiences. One idea at the time was to use a big circus top and create their own environment, where the audience did not have to obey Top Rank's dress code and the group could work out some awe-inspiring lighting effects. They would become a travelling circus. The group intended to get a huge screen, 120 feet wide and 40 feet high for their film and slide projections.

Roger: "We'll play the big cities, or anywhere and become an occasion, just like a circus. It'll be a beautiful scene... The thing is, I don't think we can go on doing what we are doing now. If we do, we'll all be on the dole."

Of course, matters were not helped by the fact that Syd really did seem to be going mad. On June 2, the Floyd played the UFO club after a two month absence. The only way to the dressing room was through the audience.

Joe Boyd: 'It was very crushed and so it was like faces two inches from your nose. So they all came by, kind of, 'Hi Joe!' 'How are you?' 'Great,' you know, and I greeted them all as they came through and the last one was Syd. And the great thing with Syd, when I had known Syd, and worked on 'Arnold Layne' and in the early days of UFO, the great thing about Syd was that if there was anything about him that you really remembered it was that he had a twinkle in his eye. I mean, he was a real eye-twinkler! He had this impish look about him, this mischievous glint, and he came by and I said 'Hi Syd' and he just kind of looked at me. I looked right in his eye and there was no twinkle. No glint. And it was like somebody had pulled the blinds, you know, nobody home. And it was a real shock. Very, very sad." It was overcrowded and very hot; among the huge crowd gathered to see the Floyd that night were Jimi Hendrix, Chas Chandler, Eric Burdon, Pete Townshend and members of the Yardbirds. 'They played like bums' the *International Times* reported the following week.

Despite Syd's condition, the group continued the relentless pursuit of pop fame and fortune and three days after *Piper* was released in Britain they returned to EMI Studios to begin work on the next album. 'Scream Thy Last Scream' was recorded on August 7 followed the next day by 'Set The Controls For The Heart Of The Sun' which presumably has Syd playing guitar on it, even though it was written by Roger (the guitar and bass were recorded simultaneously). On the 15' a session at Sound Techniques to record 'Reaction In G' was abandoned, as was one booked for the following day. Syd was getting worse and worse but the band were in denial; they were ambitious, they wanted to achieve success and it seemed at the time inconceivable that they could do this without their lead singer, lead guitarist and songwriter, so they stumbled forward, hoping he would somehow, miraculously, get better.

The Pink Floyd had to pull out of the Windsor Jazz Festival, giving as their excuse that Syd was suffering from 'nervous exhaustion', which was, for once, true. His nerves were standing on end. They contacted the psychiatrist R. D. Laing, author of *The Divided Self*, who was highly regarded at the time for his novel approach to madness. He felt that many people deemed mad were actually saner than their fellow humans, the problem being that they were placed in an untenable situation where they could not operate. As applied to Syd, this would mean that if he was allowed to just go back to being a painter, instead of having to mime to cameras and talk to idiot PR men from record companies, he would be all right. Roger drove Syd to Laing's north London clinic but Syd refused to go in. Laing later heard a tape of Syd being interviewed and said he thought Syd was "probably incurable".

The next thought was to give Syd a rest; perhaps Laing was right in thinking that the pressure of touring was causing his problems. One of the underground's leading figures was a medical doctor called Sam Hutt, famous for doing his hospital rounds dressed, not in a white coat, but in a pink Indian silk jacketeen decorated with a purple paisley pattern and with a gold Moirè silk lining worn over William Morris wallpaper pattern flares. Sam was also a musician; at the time he performed as Boeing Duveen and the Beautiful Soup, and later as Hank Wangford. At the time Syd was referred to him, Hutt was heading to the island of Formentera in the Balearics with his wife and new baby, to consider his future, whether to remain a doctor or become a professional musician. He offered to take Syd and Lynsey with him.

King and Jenner cancelled or moved all the dates set for the Floyd in August, even though their first album was due for release on August 4 and the expected thing would have been to have made as many public appearances as possible to promote it. Sam and his family, accompanied by Syd and Lynsey and Rick and Juliette Wright, who took advantage of the time off to have a Mediterranean holiday, took off for Formentera. Roger and his wife Judy went to Ibiza, the next island, and just a short ferry ride away. Unfortunately Syd seemed to get worse: he was sometimes violent and on one occasion, during a wild electric storm, Juliette reported that Syd was literally trying to climb the walls. It is possible that the lightning flashes were the trigger for an attack.

It was 50 years ago that Humphrey Osmond developed the first specific hypothesis that there was a biochemical basis for schizophrenia. Working with John Smythies at St. George's Hospital in London, he observed that chemically, mescaline is closely related to adrenaline and concluded that a fault in adrenaline metabolism in the brain might produce compounds similar to mescaline and therefore psychosis: the symptoms of disorientation and hallucinations of mescaline and schizophrenia are remarkably similar. One of these adrenaline compounds, adrenochrome, was street tested by that expert in altered states, Dr. Hunter S. Thompson who proclaimed: "That stuff makes pure mescaline seem like ginger beer". The adrenochrome high is even closer to schizophrenia psychosis than that of mescaline. Symptoms include body image disturbance and extreme thought disorder. If Syd's brain was making his own, it is no wonder he appeared mad to others.

More significantly, Smythies, working at the University of Cambridge Psychology Laboratory, reported in the *British Journal Of Psychology* that stroboscopic light served to potentiate the effects of hallucinogenic drugs like mescaline. Throughout the Fifties and Sixties there were many experiments done to examine the effect of stroboscopic lights on early experimenters with LSD. John Geiger wrote: "In one LSD experiment (Stanislav) Grof noted a dramatic change when the flashing light was introduced, and described being 'catapulted' out of his body by the flicker." Aldous Huxley noted the same effects while using a stroboscope without any drugs at all. The members of the Pink Floyd were the only ones facing the light projectors, and Syd was the only one on drugs.

The lightshow needed to flicker between 8 and 13 cycles a second (the alpha range) to increase the effect, a not unlikely occurrence given how many projectors they were using, but it would not be a constant effect which might explain why Syd's behaviour was inconsistent: sometimes utter disorientation, other times, flashes of brilliance. The extraordinary fact is that at best, it was the band's own lights that caused Syd to become disoriented on stage by exacerbating Syd's drug-induced state, and at worst, it is possible that it was the Pink Floyd's own lighting rig that drove him mad by stimulating his body's production of adrenochrome.

The band returned to play UFO one last time at its new location at the Roundhouse on September 1. The club closed on October 15, the large cost of security, high rent at the Roundhouse and increased fees for the bands – including the Pink Floyd – made it uneconomic to continue. Middle Earth, however, with permanent premises was able to continue and became the main showcase for the underground bands that were now beginning to break all over the country. Making up for lost time, the Floyd toured extensively to promote the album: first came a short Scandinavian tour, taking in Arhus, Stockholm and Copenhagen, followed by a short tour of Ireland in Belfast, Ballymena and Cork, arriving in Brussels the next day to film a television show. The next night, they were at the Speakeasy club playing to a music business audience, which must have felt relaxing after the Irish ballrooms.

On November 1 the Pink Floyd left Britain for an eight day mini-tour of America to launch their album.

Roger: "That was an amazing disaster. Syd by this time was completely off his head. We did Winterland, San Francisco. We were third on the bill to Big Brother and the Holding Company and Richie Havens. When Big Brother went on I couldn't believe it. I was expecting something way out and it was bluesy country rock. I was amazed. I expected them to be much more different. It was kind of chunka, chunka, chunka with Janis Joplin singing the blues. I was expecting something really extraordinary and mind-blowing and tripping. Compared to some of the things that English bands were doing at the time it was boring. For example the Who in a good mood or the Cream."

The group found that they had been billed as 'The Light Kings Of England' but Winterland was enormous and the tiny little lighting rig they had with them couldn't possibly fill the space so they used the same lighting men as Janis Joplin. Bands did not have their own lights in America; lighting crews were independent outfits contracted to ballrooms and clubs under their own name; the Fillmore used Joshua Lights, who were often advertised on the posters as if they were an added attraction.

Andrew King told David Parker about the main projectionist: "I remember him saying to me, 'Hey, there are such strange animals in your music!' I was thinking, 'You're fucking right, mate!'" Fortunately Syd managed to play reasonably well in San Francisco, and initially the band was able to enjoy the easy-going Californian hippie scene. At that point any band from England was regarded as visiting aristocracy and the group and their road crew found themselves surrounded by enormously friendly Californian girls and plied with more pot than they had ever seen in their lives while non-smokers Nick and Roger were introduced by Janis Joplin to the sweet-tasting delights of Southern Comfort.

As the tour progressed, however, it began to take on nightmarish aspects as Syd began to disintegrate before their very eyes. Things got off to a bad start when the group arrived in Los Angeles and found that Syd had forgotten his guitar which had to be flown up at great expense and bother from San Francisco. The Floyd's record company was Tower Records, a wholly owned American subsidiary of EMI and housed, along with EMI's main American label, Capitol Records, in the famous circular glass building at Sunset and Vine which resembled a stack of 45s on a spindle, waiting to drop onto the turntable. A Tower Records A&R man proudly showed them their HQ building, announcing "Here were are, at the centre of it all: Hollywood and Vine." Syd showed that he was still functioning with his deflating reply: "It's great to be in Las Vegas."*

The group played the newly opened Cheetah Club, housed in the old Aragon Ballroom on Pacific Ocean Park in Venice. Before they left for the States Syd had had one of his £20 perms done at Vidal Sassoon to make him look like Jimi Hendrix but he thought they had done a bad job and decided that he wanted to straighten out his curls. In the dressing room at the Cheetah, just as they were preparing to go onstage, Syd took a jar of hair gel and tipped the whole lot on his head. Next he produced a bottle of Mandrax (or more likely quaaludes, as methaqualone was called in the States) and rubbed them into his hair.* He was sitting in front of the dressing room

*This may have been the memorable occasion when an American record executive asked, 'Which one's Pink?'
*David Gilmour later commented that he "still can't believe that Syd would waste good Mandies".

make-up lights which caused the gel to began to melt and run down his face and neck until, as Roger put it, Syd looked like "like a gutted candle".

The band took the stage and apparently girls in the front row screamed with horror as Syd's lips and nostrils bubbled and ran with the gel as rivulets oozed down his cheeks, the mixed-in sleeping pills looking like tiny gobbets of flesh as if he was discomposing before their eyes in the moving lights. He detuned the strings of his guitar and stared out into space, his right hand hanging limply at his side, too out of it to sing any of the lyrics. Roger, who had to deliver the vocals for him, was so angry afterwards that he demanded that Syd be thrown out of the group on the spot. In fact Syd was probably very into the music: he detuned the strings to emulate Keith Rowe, listening to each one, blew on a whistle, and possibly thought he was participating in a free-form concert; he had always been allowed to improvise at will. I saw many AMM concerts and long periods of time often passed before anyone made any noise at all. It is possible that Syd strummed a few times during the concert, which would have seemed like a proper contribution to him in AMM mode.

For many of the crew, and some of the band, this debacle was the final straw and they abandoned themselves to the pleasures of the road, which in Los Angeles were many. They were not sleeping much because of jet lag and were staying at the Tropicana Motel on Santa Monica Blvd, home of many rock and roll groups including half of the Mothers of Invention, and very much groupie central in the days before the Hyatt House hotel on Sunset Boulevard became 'the Riot House.' It was always interesting to see who accompanied members of the band and crew to breakfast at Duke's 24-hour coffee shop next door for breakfast. As a consequence, some of the band and crew had to report to James Pringle House's VD clinic as soon as they returned to London.

On November 5 they were on Pat Boone's television show to promote their new single, 'Apples And Oranges' and though Syd mimed perfectly during rehearsals he refused to move when the cameras went live.

Roger: "We did the Pat Boone show, and we were taping the show, and he would do the run-through and Syd would stand with his Telecaster with silver bits all over it and mime happily. 'Cut, cut, we are going to do it now'... He knew perfectly well what was going on, he was just being crazy and they did four or five takes like that. Eventually I mimed it."

Despite this, Pat Boone chose Syd to talk to and asked him an inane question about what kind of things he liked. Syd fixed him with a *Night Of The Living Dead*-style stare and pondered the question. The rest of the band waited for what seemed like an eternity, buttocks clenched in horror as they saw their American career going down the tubes. Eventually Syd said 'America', which made the all-American audience holler and shout their approval. On Dick Clark's *American Bandstand* Syd half-heartedly mimed, as if catatonic, through 'Apples And Oranges' and 'See Emily Play'. For Perry Como's show, it was Rick who had to mime 'Matilda Mother'. After this, Andrew King finally accepted reality and cancelled a *Beach Party* TV appearance and a New York engagement at the Cheetah Club and put the group on a plane home. Before leaving Syd managed to fall into the Tropicana pool fully clothed and just abandoned his wet clothes in his room when leaving for LAX.

The Pink Floyd did what most bands did in those days: they churned out singles in order to boost their gig fees. On November 17, 'Apples And Oranges' backed by 'Paintbox' was released, recorded before the ill-fated American tour. In a *Melody Maker* interview in December to promote it, Syd sounded surprisingly articulate: "It's unlike anything we've done before. It's a new sound. Got a lot of guitar in it. It's a happy song, and it's got a touch of Christmas. It's about a girl who I just saw walking round town, in Richmond. The 'apples and oranges' bit is the refrain in the middle."

By this time Syd's inability to play live had undermined the band's reputation. Their gigs were terrible and bookings began to fall off. They still had supporters such as John Peel who had them on his *Top Gear* show on September 30, and again on December 19, but at the latter show Syd 'freaked out' and the BBC blacklisted the Floyd for a time after that. Still the band kept on playing; though it was obvious that Syd was not going to improve, they remained in denial. Even when they collected Syd in the Bentley one day and he climbed into the car in full make-up wearing something close to drag they didn't say a word. The Pink Floyd's way was to ignore it. Clearly things could not continue as they were.

Nick Mason told a French interviewer: "Contrary to everything that was said, things were very simple. It was getting harder to work with Syd, because we couldn't reach

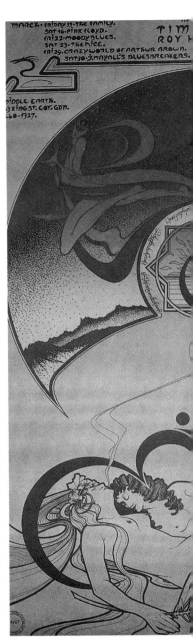

Above: The Pink Floyd at Middle Earth in Covent Garden.

him. He was getting more absent every time, in both senses of the word. He would forget to appear at the gigs. When we were at a radio broadcast he left the studio without warning. He wasn't showing up at the rehearsals anymore. In a word, he wasn't in the band. This situation was gradually becoming more obvious and, one day, Rick, Roger and me, became aware that we couldn't keep playing live if Syd continued in Pink Floyd, since he didn't want to show up in public with us. The thought of breaking up with Syd disturbed us. But it ended up happening and we regret that."

Blackhill had booked the Pink Floyd onto a UK package tour starring the Jimi Hendrix Experience; a series of one-nighters with seven bands on the bill doing two sets a night each for three weeks in the old Denmark Street music biz tradition. At least they didn't have a dog act or any hoofers with them but it meant that there were seven sets of equipment onstage, waiting to be dragged into place by an overworked road crew. The Floyd were billed with Eire Apparent, the Nice, Amen Corner, the Move and the Outer Limits with DJ Pete Drummond, opening at the Royal Albert Hall on November 14. The first half was closed by Amen Corner and the Pink Floyd opened the second. They had quarter of an hour to do their show, resulting, on some nights, like at the Albert Hall, in one long improvised instrumental filling the allotted time.

Roger: "It was really fantastic. The last of the great one-nighters." The tour played Bournemouth, Sheffield, Liverpool, Coventry, Portsmouth, Cardiff, Bristol, Blackpool and Manchester. A quick flight to Belfast, where they went down really well – Nick Mason: "They were all wild ravers!" – then Chatham, Brighton, Nottingham, Newcastle and Glasgow. The musicians all travelled in a coach, while Hendrix drove ahead in a car though he sometimes joined the others, sitting at the back of the bus, cracking jokes, dubbing the Floyd's eccentric guitarist "Laughing Syd Barrett". Though Syd had Lynsey with him, he sometimes failed to materialise at showtime so David O'List from the Nice stood in for him. One time, Peter Jenner managed to head Syd off at a train station to prevent him escaping.

Nick: "It's easy now to look back on 'the past' and try and give it some sort of shape and form, but at the time you're just… you're in a total state of confusion muddling about because you're trying to be in this band and be successful or make it work, and things aren't working out and you don't really understand why. You can't believe that someone's deliberately trying to screw it up and yet the other half of you is saying 'This man's crazy – he's trying to *destroy me!*' It gets very personal, you get very worked up into a state of extreme rage. I mean, obviously there was some incredible moments of… clarity, where you realise that things are not right – like the wonderful American tour which will live forever. Syd detuning his guitar all the way through one number, striking the string and detuning the guitar, which is very modern but very difficult for a band to follow or play with. And, other occasions where he more or less just ceased playing and stood there, leaving us to muddle along as best we could. And times like that, you think 'What we need is someone else!' Or at least some help."

The band stumbled on to Christmas. The last big freak out of the year was the *Christmas On Earth Revisited* event held at Olympia, on December 22, with Jimi Hendrix, the Move, Eric Burdon and the Animals, Soft Machine and the Pink Floyd. The Floyd came on at 5 am, Syd was completely out of it again, and as far as the band was concerned, the Summer of Love staggered to a close. Nick Mason wrote of their dilemma that they were no longer in denial about the need to replace Barrett, but Syd was an old friend, they really did not want to hurt him but they had no choice.

'This man's crazy – he's trying to destroy me!' It gets very personal, you get very worked up into a state of extreme rage.'

Nick Mason

CHAPTER NINE
DAVID JOINS

Right: The brief
five-man line up
of Pink Floyd,
early 1968. Syd
fades from view.

CHAPTER NINE
DAVID JOINS

When Roger and Syd went to study in London, David Gilmour remained in Cambridge and started Jokers Wild. In 1966, when the band seemed to have reached a dead end David, together with fellow Cambridge musicians drummer Willie Wilson and bassist Ricky Wills took up the offer of a gig in a Marbella night club. When that job finished they moved on to Paris. At first they called themselves Bullitt.

David: "I can't remember why we called it that. I was living with my band in France and we just thought of a name, but as we approached the Summer of Love it just didn't seem to be appropriate!" Consequently in Paris they became Flowers, because their manager thought they needed a name more in keeping with the times. Flowers got a regular weekend residency at Le Bilboquet, the famous Left Bank nightclub at 13 rue Benoit, a home to Billie Holiday, Miles Davis, Kenny Clarke, Duke Ellington, Art Blakey, Dizzy Gillespie, Lionel Hampton and Charlie Parker in the great days of Paris jazz.

David: "We struggled to get by, living this nomadic existence in France on 50 francs a night each – three or four quid back then, and that only a couple of times a week." The trio lived in a succession of cheap Left Bank hotels, staying two to a room and often had to spend all night in a Paris bar, nursing one glass of beer, because they had nowhere to stay and no money. David stayed in Paris for a year.

He kept up with old friends in the Pink Floyd, visiting them in the studio in May 1967 when they were recording 'See Emily Play' and then, in August, he heard *The Piper At The Gates Of Dawn* LP. He told Phil Sutcliffe: "It sounded terrific and I was sick with jealousy. I'd been ill. Malnutrition, strangely enough, the hospital gave me sugar to suck on." Gilmour and his cohorts in Flowers paid their hotel bill on the weekends, after being paid by Le Bilboquet, but that only left enough money to buy food for a few days, and then they would run out and sometimes had to go without. "Extreme pigheadedness and stubbornness can be both great qualities and character faults," he said. "I hung on too long in France, but in September '67 I thought, 'I've had enough. I'm going home'."

The three of them went to one or two people who owed them money and threatened them with violence if they didn't pay up. At one booking agency they took equipment from the office that they thought they could sell after the agent made the usual excuses. On the way to Calais they ran out of money for petrol for their battered old Ford Thames van. They stopped at a building site and siphoned diesel into their tank. Willie Wilson warned that although the van would run on this mixture of diesel and petrol, it would not start again, so when they reached Calais at 3am, they kept the engine running all night as they waited for the first ferry of the day. Once on board they were made to switch off the motor and sure enough, at Dover they had to push the van

Bottom: Pink Floyd
Mark II, 1968.
L-R: David Gilmour,
Nick Mason,
Roger Waters,
Rick Wright.

off the ferry onto the dock. David: "I felt a bit defeated at that point." He told Ricky and Willie that he wasn't going back to Cambridge – "That would have been one defeatist stage too far" – he would stay in London and try and make it in the music business.

David took a job as a van driver for Ossie Clarke and Alice 'No Pants' Pollock's Kings Road dress shop Quorum and spent his evenings hanging around the clubs and getting to know the music scene, hoping to put together a new group. Then, on December 6, at a Floyd gig at the Royal College of Art, he was sounded out about joining the Floyd.

David: "Nick actually came to me and sort of said 'Nudge, nudge... if such and such happened, and if this, and if that, would you be interested in it?' and went through that whole thing in a fairly roundabout way, suggesting that this might come off at some point. And then just after Christmas, right after their Olympia gig, I actually got a phone call... where I was staying. I didn't actually have a phone, or they didn't know it, but they sent a message through someone else that they knew that knew me, for me to get in touch for taking the job, so to speak. There was no real discussion, or any meetings to think about it or any auditions or anything like that. They just said, 'Did I want to?' and I said 'Yes', and it was as simple as that."

Rick Wright told Q magazine: "When Syd left Pink Floyd we actually asked Jeff Beck to join, he was our first choice. He was doing OK at the time so he turned us down." Beck would have been a more commercial but unlikely choice, since he was already well-known and would have immediately upped their profile and fees, but David

Gilmour was in fact the best possible candidate they could have found.

David: "They just basically asked me because I was probably the only other person they really knew fairly well that could sing and play guitar, and came from a reasonably similar background, so that we knew that we'd probably get on reasonably well and could communicate, and they know what I could do – I mean I think the other person they had in mind was Jeff Beck, which would have been slightly different."

Nick: "During a month, the five of us rehearsed together. Our idea was to adopt the Beach Boys' formula, in which Brian Wilson got together with the band on stage when he wanted to. We absolutely wanted to preserve Syd in Pink Floyd one way or the other. But he let himself be influenced by some people, who kept repeating he was the only talent in the band and should pursue a solo career."

This referred of course to Peter Jenner and Andrew King who still thought that Syd was the only creative mind in the band and that the Pink Floyd would go nowhere without him. In fact, in the long term Syd might well have held them back with his love of pop star glamour but we will never know. By now Syd was virtually impossible to communicate with, they had no way of knowing what he was thinking or what he wanted. He was an old friend and they found themselves in an almost impossible dilemma.

Roger: "Syd turned into a very strange person. Whether he was sick in any way or not is not for us to say in these days of dispute about the nature of madness. All I know is that he was fucking murder to live and work with."

Initially the band saw themselves as having three options: the five piece where Syd could join them onstage if he felt like it; Syd not playing with them but staying home and writing for them, thus remaining part of the group, and a third where Syd left the group and was replaced by David. It only took a handful of gigs to show that they could no longer allow Syd to appear onstage with them: he fixed the audience with a glassy stare, and if he touched his guitar at all, it was to detune the strings and strum rattling discords. Sometimes the strings would fall off altogether. As they were not a free-form experimental group, this did not enhance either their playing or their reputation.

It was difficult for Syd as well; at the band meeting where the idea of David joining the line-up had been proposed it had been made very clear to Syd that no disagreement was allowed. Technically David was the second guitarist and backup vocalist but as far as Syd was concerned, his old friend was, as Nick Mason put it, "an interloper". Syd went through the motions of playing, as if he refused to get involved in this absurd charade, but as he contributed less and less, the need for his replacement became more and more clear.

This was the time of Syd's brilliant comment on the band and his situation within it. At the school hall rehearsal room they used in north London, Syd attempted to teach the group a new song called 'Have You Got It Yet?' Each time they reached the chorus, Syd changed the arrangement. When he sang, 'Have you got it yet?' they all chorused back, 'No, no.' It lasted for an hour, before they realised that Syd was simply making them look foolish.

Nick: "So we were teaching Dave the numbers with the idea that we were going to be a five piece. But Syd came in with some new material. The song went 'Have you got it yet?' and he kept changing it so no-one could learn it."

Roger: "It was a real act of mad genius. The interesting thing about it was that I didn't suss it out at all. I stood there for about an hour while he was singing "Have you got it yet?" trying to explain that he was changing it all the time so I couldn't follow it. He'd sing, 'Have you got it yet?' and I'd sing 'No, no!' Terrific!"

The others had all seen David in his various groups so there had been no need for him to play for them, but in order for him to become part of their recording contract he had to do an audition at EMI Studios. This he passed easily, first of all playing in the Hendrix mould, before showing how he could both sing and play like Syd; not a direct imitation, but in the same style. This was not surprising since he and Syd grew up together musically and he knew every aspect of Syd's playing inside out. The Pink Floyd's contract with EMI was formally revised to include David on March 18, 1968.

David had seen two or three of the Floyd's gigs before being asked to join and had been shocked at how poor they sounded. It was obvious that the band could not carry on as it was; they were static, just marking time. David joining the band coincided, of course, with Roger taking over Syd's role as leader of the group. David, as the new boy, and the youngest member by that crucial two years, came in for a lot of criticism from Waters.

David: "Roger assumed leadership of Pink Floyd because he was leadership material. He was bossy and pushy, and I'm very grateful that he was there to take the reins. But I felt like a new boy. And Roger, the jolly old soul that he was, rubbed it in to me: both the younger bit and the new-boy bit." So much so, in fact, that after his first few days David left the band because Roger was making his life so difficult; fortunately a reconciliation was effected.

The five man Pink Floyd line-up was short-lived: they played the University of Aston in Birmingham, the Saturday Dance Date at the Winter Gardens Pavilion in Weston-super-Mare, two evening shows at Lewis Town Hall and a gig on the pier at Hastings. The end of Syd's live career with the Pink Floyd came about on January 26, 1968 when the band set off to play the University of Southampton as support to Tyrannosaurus Rex and the Incredible String Band. As their white Bentley headed down Ladbroke Grove from a business meeting to pick him up, someone asked, 'Shall we go and pick up Syd?' and someone – generally thought to have been Roger – replied, 'Oh, let's not!' and off they went to Southampton without him. The five-piece had lasted for only four gigs. This left David with the unenviable task of performing as lead vocalist and lead guitarist.

The band never told Gilmour to 'Play like Syd Barrett'; if that was what they were looking for they would never have considered Jeff Beck for the position. It so happened that there were many similarities in style between Syd and David's playing and, as they were still playing Syd's material, and as David was a great mimic, he opted to play in a manner similar to Barrett until the group had developed some fresh, non-Syd, material: 'I had to fit in with his style to an extent because his songs were so rigidly structured around it.'

Gilmour told Nicky Horne: 'The first six months that I was in the band I really didn't feel confident enough to actually start playing myself – I sat there mostly playing just rhythm guitar and I suppose, to be honest, at the time trying to sound a bit like Syd. But that didn't last very long – I mean, it was obvious the group had to change into something completely different and they hadn't asked me to join to sound exactly like Syd, but I mean – the numbers they were doing were still Syd's numbers mostly. Consequently there's that kind of a fixed thing in your head of how they have been played previously, and that kind of, makes it very much harder for you to strike out on your own and do it exactly how you would do it… and you haven't got a clue how you would do it really because there's already an imprinted thing in your brain of how the guitar is played on those things. Consequently it did take some time before I started getting into actually being a member of the band and feeling free to impose my own... guitar-playing style on it.

Accusations from Barrett fans that David was somehow an impostor who was imitating Syd's style naturally angered him: "The facts of the matter are that I was using an echo box years before Syd was. I also used slide. I also taught Syd quite a lot about guitar. I mean, people saying that I pinched his style, when our backgrounds are so similar...yet we spent a lot of times as teenagers listening to the same music. Our influences are pretty much the same – and I was a couple of streets ahead of him at the time and was teaching him to play Stones' riffs every lunchtime for a year at technical college. That kind of thing's bound to get my back up – especially if you don't check it."

Syd, for his part, was confused and angry. He had never seen the others as merely his backing group, or himself as the leader of the band; he was devoted to the band and couldn't really understand why he was no longer in it. When asked about his leaving by Mick Watts, he said: "It wasn't really a war. I suppose it was really just a matter of being a little offhand about things. We didn't feel there was one thing which was gonna make the decision at the minute. I mean, we did split up, and there was a lot of trouble. I don't think the Pink Floyd had any trouble, but I had an awful scene, probably self-inflicted.'

Meanwhile, the rest of the band breathed a sigh of relief.

Nick: "After Syd, Dave was the difference between light and dark. He was absolutely into form and shape and he introduced that into the wilder numbers we'd created. We became far less difficult to enjoy."

Rick agreed: "[Dave] was much more of a straight blues guitarist than Syd, of course, and very good. That changed the direction, although he did try to reproduce Syd's style live."

SAUCERFUL OF SECRETS

The first order of business was to complete the second Pink Floyd album; something which had become impossible in the final months of 1967 because of Syd's unpredictable behaviour. They already had a few tracks in hand from a two day recording session at De Lane Lea studios in Kingsway on October 9-12, 1967 when they recorded Rick's 'Remember A Day' with a nice slide solo by Syd, and Barrett's extraordinary 'Jugband Blues'* and 'Vegetable Man' – the latter written in the studio when Syd sat in the corner and scribbled it down. It was when the band saw the words, and realised that it was a description of himself, that they began to get seriously worried.

They also had an unfinished version of 'Set The Controls For The Heart Of The Sun,' first started back in August 1967. On January 11, it was resurrected and several sessions were devoted to working on it. David overdubbed most of the guitar on the final version but just enough of Syd remains – Gilmour: "A tiny bit" – for it to stand as the only recorded example of the five-man Pink Floyd line-up, albeit through the marvels of multi-track tape. This was Roger's best composition to date; he spent four months working on it before presenting it to the band.

Unsure of himself as a lyricist, he used Syd's technique and appropriated all the words from ancient Chinese poetry: The line "Little by little/ the night turns around" is the second line of an untitled poem by the late Tang period poet Li Shang-yin (AD 813 – 858) which reads: "Watch little by little the night turn around." Another of Li Shang-yin's untitled poems is the source of "One inch of love is one inch of shadow" and "Counting the leaves which tremble at dawn" comes from his poem 'Willow'. The poem, 'Don't Go Out Of The Door' by Li Ho (AD 790 – 816) provided the line "witness the man who raved at the wall/ as he wrote his question to heaven" – and so on. The title of the number is taken from Michael Moorcock's sci-fi novel *Fireclown**

Roger: "It was one of my first songs of Pink Floyd, and one of my first compositions. Actually, it was my first composition to be recorded. It is a piece of Chinese poetry. In truth, the only phrase of mine is the heading. All the remaining lyrics were practically lifted from this Chinese poetry."

David: "By the time Syd left the ball had definitely stopped rolling. We had to start it all over again. *Saucerful Of Secrets*, the first album without him, was the start back on the road to some kind of return. It was the album we began building from. The whole conception of *Saucerful Of Secrets* has nothing to do with what Syd believed in or liked."

There are reports that Syd sat, guitar in hand, in the lobby of EMI Studios, day after

*The soundtrack to an obscure colour film short showing the group (with Syd) miming the song in a studio setting – Wright and Waters playing wind instruments during the demented Salvation Army break. The clip was made by, of all things, the Central Office of Information.
*Also published as *The Winds Of Limbo*.

Above: After Syd left, Roger Waters took over as the band's main songwriter.

day, waiting for the band to invite him in to contribute. It is hard to imagine that they would have been un-moved by this and not have at least installed him in the control booth.

Saucerful was a transitional album, part Floyd Mark I, part Mark II, and most of all, a transition between a singles band with a penchant for extended avant-garde improvisation to a more melodic band interested in creating sound sculpture and atmospheres. Another factor to contend with was producer Norman 'Hurricane' Smith who was still intent on producing three minute singles for EMI. The idea of a band that didn't release singles was beyond his comprehension and it soon became clear that his commercial pop approach was anathema to their non-commercial 'progressive rock' direction.

Rick: "We were pretty cocky by now and told him 'If you don't want to produce it, go away.'"

The lengthy title track instrumental could have easily not happened. The band had put together a reasonable second album so Smith graciously allowed them a bit of space at the end of recording to do what they liked as a reward.

Roger: "It was the actual title track of *A Saucerful Of Secrets* that gave us our second breath. We had finished the whole album. The company wanted the whole thing to be a follow-up to the first album but what we wanted to do was this longer piece. And it was given to us by the company like sweeties after we'd finished. We could do what we liked with the last twelve minutes."

The track gave them new confidence.

Roger: "It was the first thing we'd done without Syd that we thought was any good."

According to David, Nick and Roger approached the song "as an architectural

diagram, in dynamic forms rather than in any sort of musical form, with peaks and troughs. That's what it was about. It wasn't music for beauty's sake, or for emotion's sake. It never had a storyline. Though for years afterwards we used to get letters from people saying what they thought it meant. Scripts for movies sometimes too."

Gilmour told Guitar World: "'A Saucerful' was inspired when Roger and Nick began drawing weird shapes on a piece of paper. We then composed music based on the structure of the drawing… We tried to write the music around the peaks and valleys of the art. My role, I suppose, was to try and make it a bit more musical, and to help create a balance between formlessness and structure, disharmony and harmony."

They created the track in the studio from scratch, improvising and building the layers of sound until they got it right. It was a thrilling, exciting, experience but not everyone liked it. Norman Smith was appalled.

Rick: "He just couldn't – he didn't – understand. He said, 'Well, I think it's rubbish. It won't sell a single copy, but go ahead and do it, if you want' sort of thing. Whereas we all believed it was gonna be one of the best things we'd ever put onto record. Which I think it was at that time." Everyone within the band recognised that they had done something significant with 'Saucerful'. Nick said that it was the key to "helping sort out the direction we were going to move in. It contains ideas that were well ahead of the period, and very much a route that I think we have followed. Even without using a lot of elaborate technique, without being particularly able in our own right, finding something we can do individually that other people haven't tried… like provoking the most extraordinary sounds from a piano by scratching 'round inside it."

David: "That was the first clue to our direction forwards, from there. If you take 'Saucerful of Secrets', the track 'Atom Heart Mother', then the track 'Echoes' – all lead quite logically towards *Dark Side Of The Moon.*

After they finished recording, Norman Smith told Floyd roadie Pete Watts: "After this album they will really have to knuckle down and get something together." There was never a sudden break with Smith; no big argument, but after Syd left he seemed to be less and less interested in the direction the band were taking. Though he had found Syd difficult, if not almost impossible to deal with, he always saw him as a commercial artist and could see no one else in the band likely to write a chart topper.

The professional partnership between band and producer drifted apart naturally; the Floyd appreciated how much Smith had taught them about using a studio; many producers at that time were very secretive about the mysteries of the mixing desk and

'He just couldn
understand. He
think it's rubbis
a single copy, b
do it, if you wan
Whereas we al
gonna be one o
we'd ever put o

Rick Wright

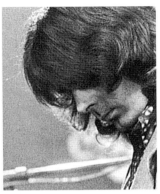

the tangle of patchcords that were used to connect the Dolby sound reduction units making that end of the studio look like a telephone exchange. He allowed them to watch during tape reductions and mixing and let them produce a track he had no empathy for – 'A Saucerful Of Secrets' – themselves. By the time of *Ummagumma* a year later the Floyd felt confident that they no longer needed Smith's expertise.

Saucerful ends with Barrett's remarkable 'Jugband Blues', recorded in October 1967 when he was still relatively active in the band, with its eerily knowledgeable lyrics about his own condition, as if he could see what was happening to him and yet could do nothing about it. Addressing the band he sang: "It's awfully considerate of you to think of me here/ And I'm most obliged to you for making it clear that I'm not here." The last line of the album, the last line of Syd's career with Pink Floyd asked: "And what exactly is a joke?" It is one of his greatest songs, and one of his most experimental tracks.

One of the few conversations I had with Syd that I can remember anything about was regarding the Beatles track 'A Day In The Life'. I had been at several of the sessions for it and Syd was intrigued to hear about Paul McCartney's instructions to the orchestra to play 24 bars, beginning at the lowest note in their instrument's register, and ending 24 bars later at its highest. How they got there was up to them. The orchestra were horrified not to have a written score but managed it. I think that this was in Syd's mind for 'Jugband Blues' when he demanded that Norman Smith bring in a brass band who were instructed to "play whatever you want."

Smith had produced an album by the Salvation Army Band of north London and dutifully brought them in but he could not bring himself to allow them to play free-form. Normally he and Syd had little to do with each other; Syd went his own way and changed his songs and music at every whim, much to Norman's irritation. This time, however, it boiled over into a full scale row. After half an hour Syd got fed up and walked out, leaving Smith to finish the track as best he could. He got them to play a bit of free-form, and a bit of oom-pah music as well, just to make his point. The pointless stereo swings from the left to right channels were also his, the Floyd were only present for the mono mixing.

On February 12 and 13, as part of the *Saucerful* sessions, the Floyd recorded Rick's 'It Would Be So Nice' and Roger's 'Julia Dream'; originally respectively titled 'It Should Be So Nice' and 'Doreen's Dream', the latter being the first Pink Floyd song to be recorded with David Gilmour on guitar and vocals. It was released as a single on April 12 in advance of the album but went nowhere. The band was not surprised. Nick Mason later commented: "Fucking awful that record wasn't it? At that period we had no direction." Without Barrett, they were not a singles band – a fact brought home to them even more clearly with their next single – their last for more than ten years – 'Point Me At The Sky' and 'Careful With That Axe, Eugene' released on December 17 that same year, 1968, which again did not sell and the Americans did not even bother to release.

Peter Jenner and Andrew King had always backed Syd as the creative force in the Pink Floyd and just could not see the group surviving without him. There was little evidence that the others could write; the only example was Roger's appalling 'Take Up Thy Stethoscope And Walk' on *Piper*. The pair had also backed Syd in his struggle to remain in the group, assuring him that he was the creative genius. It was inevitable then, that when Roger, Nick and Rick decided that Syd had to go, there would be dissension from Jenner and King when they heard about it. At first the group did not tell them that they were no longer taking Barrett to gigs, nor did they reveal the addition of Gilmour to their line-up which came as a complete surprise to the management team.

As the Pink Floyd management was a six-way partnership, the band members did not have a clear majority, but according to Nick the breakup, when it came, was remarkably civil. Peter and Andrew opted to manage Syd and did not feel that the rest of the band stood a chance. A meeting was held on March 2 with all parties present (including Syd) and the six-way partnership was dissolved, with Jenner and King keeping Blackhill Enterprises and an agreement made that they would receive 20% in perpetuity of all income arising from recordings made during their tenure. The band took over the hire purchase payments on their equipment, and with the band's bookings already being arranged by the Bryan Morrison Agency, they asked Morrison to manage them.

Nick remembers that Syd's contribution to the meeting was to suggest that two girl saxophone players be added to the Floyd lineup.

CHAPTER TEN
MEET THE
NEW BOSS

CHAPTER TEN
MEET THE NEW BOSS

It was Roger who had finally forced the issue over Syd, and Roger who took over as band leader. This was largely by default: David was the new boy and not in a position to assert himself, and both Rick and Nick preferred to keep their heads down. Roger was a good organiser, forceful and determined, some people even said he was rude. He had made this his career, and was determined that Pink Floyd should overcome this set back, major as it was.

David: "He was the one who had the courage to drive Syd out, because he realised that as long as Syd was in the band, they wouldn't keep it together, the chaos factor was too great. Roger looked up to Syd and he always felt very guilty about the fact that he'd blown out his mate." Syd was well aware of this. According to his sister, years afterwards, it was Roger that Syd railed against in his fits of madness, howling his name. Nor did Syd just go away quietly: he thoroughly disconcerted David by standing next to the stage at Middle Earth in his frills and makeup, glaring at the new guitarist, making it clear that he thought his friend had usurped his position, and at a gig at Imperial College, Syd had to be told firmly that he couldn't play with his old band. Deep down, a confused Barrett didn't really understand why he was no longer in the band.

The band had to learn how to survive their most profound line-up change. There were precious few examples for them to learn from: Brian Jones was not yet fired from the Rolling Stones, Fleetwood Mac's extreme makeover was years ahead, and the Yardbirds' succession of guitar players, Clapton, Beck and Page, was not exactly comparable. Ominously, the Spencer Davis Group had virtually foundered when focal point Steve Winwood left to form Traffic the previous year.

Fortunately Pink Floyd had always played down individual personality in favour of the group image and photographs tended to show all of them. The lightshows had always meant that the audience never had a clear view of them, unless they were right up front, so even early on, the Floyd was more of an idea, some kind of entity, rather than four distinct personalities.

Roger was by now a married man, living with wife Judy in a terraced house on New North Road in Islington, then a run down neighbourhood in north London that was slowly being gentrified. He bought the house in 1968 for £8,000 and renovated himself, using his architectural training. He converted the basement into a large kitchen where his Burmese cats liked to spend their time near the heat and food. This rehabilitation all took some time as Pink Floyd had a heavy schedule and by 1970 they were still living in the basement. Eventually he sanded and polished the wooden floors, bought tasteful Scandinavian furniture and created a home. The kitchen featured a large black and white photograph of Arsenal scoring against Derby; Roger was an Arsenal fanatic and all recording sessions had to be postponed if a match was

Below: Roger
releases his
aggression on his
J. Arthur Rank
gong during
'Careful With
That Axe, Eugene'.

on and whenever possible he watched the team from the North Terrace.

At the end of the garden Roger rebuilt a shed to provide a soundproof demo studio for himself and a larger space next door for Judy to use as a sculpture studio and to house a kiln for her pottery. Judy was an accomplished potter who was then working as a teacher of painting and sculpture. Judy Trim was Roger's childhood girlfriend from Cambridge whom some people thought he had married to spite his possessive mother who had not wanted him to settle down with a girlfriend. As is so often the case, Judy was a younger version of his mother: they were schoolteachers, disliked rock 'n' roll, and were supporters of the radical left. Above all, they were both powerful women.

Floyd insiders marvelled at the way Judy bossed Roger around. Peter Jenner told Nick Schaffner: "On the one hand, Roger was extremely tough and strong and held the band together after Syd left. At the same time, he was weak – always very influenced by his women. His first wife, Judy, was an extreme leftie, a Trot. When he was with her, Pink Floyd money was spent on buying rows of houses to be let at economic rents to the deserving poor, in the best tradition of the English upper-middle class benefactors."

In the first flush of their success Roger had bought himself an E-type Jaguar, one of the most beautiful English cars ever built, but his socialist guilt won out and a few weeks later he replaced it with a Mini. Despite the conflicts caused by success, there is no doubt that Roger and Judy were very close and that when they broke up, just after

Dark Side Of The Moon, it was an extremely painful experience for both of them.

When *A Saucerful of Secrets* was released on June 21, 1968, most people recognised it as an 'interim' album but were enthusiastic about the new direction that the title track showed they were taking. Much of the album was regarded as filler and various members of the band later agreed that some of the tracks were not their best work.

Rick: "I cringe at some of my songs – such as 'Remember A Day'. We were pretty amateurish at the time, but I don't think it was just my stuff that doesn't sound so good now. Something like 'Corporal Clegg', which was one of Roger's songs, is just as bad. Syd was the songwriter and then we came in and had to take over the songwriting and it was a lot of responsibility to assume. We could never write like Syd, we never had the imagination to come out with the kind of lyrics he did."

Unfortunately the outcome of this was that the other band members now seemed resigned to the fact that they were not good at lyrics and allowed Roger to take control in this area. Roger had supreme belief in his ability as a songwriter and years later even claimed to be one of the top five wordsmiths in the business. In these early days this blind self-confidence was needed to help the shattered group find a new identity. Once established, however, he was disinclined to allow the others to develop their own voice, and Gilmour and Wright both let him write lyrics to their music.

David: "I've never had the belief in myself in that direction, and I've let myself be dominated by Roger. Never argued with him having his idea for an album and me backing off saying, 'OK, you do them, I don't do this really'." This, of course, stored up resentment and later caused trouble when Roger got the idea that he alone was Pink Floyd, forgetting that the band was composed of largely anonymous musicians and that, with one or two exceptional songs, the fans were not very interested in the lyrics anyway. But in 1968, Waters' firm hand was just what the band needed.

FREE IN THE PARK

The first large free concert held in Britain was organised by the ever-idealistic Blackhill Enterprises who were still on good enough terms with Pink Floyd to convince them to play at the Cockpit in Hyde Park on June 29, 1968. They headlined the Midsummer High Weekend with Jethro Tull and Roy Harper as support. Jenner and King had to use the old boy network and enlist the help of two Members of Parliament to persuade the Bailiff of the Royal Parks to give them permission. The Ministry of Works was not so sure and said: "We're a little fearful that it might attract the wrong element. There's enough vandalism in the Royal Parks as it is." But the Floyd allied his fears, saying: "Our music is very soothing. If any litter bins get kicked in it won't be because of us." The event was a terrific success.

John Peel said, "I always claim that the best outdoor event that I've ever been to was the Pink Floyd concert in Hyde Park, when I hired a boat and rowed out, and I lay on the bottom of the boat, in the way that we hippies did, in the middle of the Serpentine, and just listened to the band play, and their music then, as I think now, suited the open air perfectly. It was... it sounds ludicrous now, it's the kind of thing you can get away with saying at the time and which is now, in these harsher times sounds a bit silly... but I mean it was like a religious experience, it was marvellous. They played 'A Saucerful Of Secrets' and things... they just seemed to fill the whole sky and everything y'know? And to coincide perfectly with the water and the lapping of the water and the trees and everything. It just seemed to be the perfect event. I think that it was the nicest concert I've ever been to."

One of the reasons for this might have been due to it not occurring to Blackhill to construct a VIP area in front of the stage, so there was a genuine contact with the audience.

Nick: "The one in '68 was wonderful because it was much more of a picnic in the park than a mini-Woodstock. A lovely day. It was important for us too because it reminded us of our, uh, roots – whether spurious or not. They were our roots – not personally, but as an enterprise. We were the house band."

Pink Floyd was now quite well established, they had a couple of albums out and enough gigs to make a decent living. They had a professional road manager in the shape of Peter Watts and when it became apparent that the equipment was too much for one man to set up, Alan Styles joined him as an assistant. Alan had previously looked after the punts outside the Mill pub in Cambridge and was celebrated for his long hair and tight trousers. He fitted right in.

An American tour was booked for the summer of 1968 and shortly before the band left for New York, their booking agent, Bryan Morrison, who had been managing their

affairs ever since the break with Blackhill, arrived with a new set of contracts, saying that the American tour paperwork demanded another agency agreement. Roger, cleverly, thought something was amiss and on behalf of the group, only signed for the six weeks of the tour. Sure enough, the music business lived up to its reputation and two days later, it was announced in the press that the booking agency and management side of the Bryan Morrison Agency had been sold to NEMS for £40,000. The Floyd's agent was now Vic Lewis, an old-fashioned Denmark Street type who had taken over NEMS after Brian Epstein's death.

Though they were signed for the summer, the fact that Morrison had not been able to get the Floyd to sign a long term management contract meant that the group had considerable leverage to make a new deal. Steve O'Rourke, who had acted on their behalf at the Morrison Agency, was released from his post to become the Floyd's personal manager[*] and NEMS would take over their bookings in exchange for a cash advance. The group was pleased with the new arrangements.

Rick: "At last we've got a really good agency. We're doing as much work as we want to. There's plenty of it, too much in fact... one or two a week is really all we want."

Pink Floyd arrived in New York on July 4 to begin their second American tour but yet again found that their management had fallen foul of US regulations; work permits could only be issued out of the country so they were forced to go to Montreal until the problem was fixed. David's guitar went missing en route to their first gig in Chicago forcing him to buy the Fender Stratocaster he'd always wanted. He also bought a Fender pedal steel from a junk shop on this trip which was to shortly appear on their recordings.

After playing Chicago and Detroit, they found themselves staying at the Hotel Chelsea in New York with both band and crew squeezing into two dilapidated rooms. The Floyd had a three night residency at Steve Paul's Scene, a groupie club headquarters in a cellar at 46th Street and Sixth Avenue, which rather set the tone for the whole trip.

Rick: "In the summer of '68, there were groupies everywhere; they'd come and look after you like a personal maid, do your washing, sleep with you and leave with a dose of the clap."

Even Nick Mason boasts of staggering back to the Chelsea after the show with one of the girls from *Hair.* The band played the Avalon in San Francisco and the Shrine Auditorium in Los Angeles, but enlarged their audience by performing at a number of summer festivals including Philadelphia with the Who and the Troggs (although the concert was abandoned midway through the Floyd's set because of wet weather); the three day Sky River Rock Festival in Sultan, Washington, with Kaleidoscope, Muddy Waters, Santana, Country Joe & the Fish, John Fahey, Steppenwolf and the Youngbloods, and – on the last night of the tour – in Rochester, Michigan for the Oakland Pop Festival at the university with MC5, Howlin' Wolf and Procol Harum. The band did not particularly like festivals because the audience's mind was on other things: having fun, having sex, taking drugs, and anticipating other groups. The Floyd preferred, whenever possible, to be the only band on the bill; then they knew the audience was there just to listen to them and for no other purpose.

The band was still in no position to live by recording alone and so they had to solve the biggest problem of their live performance: they couldn't reproduce their album material on stage, and, in Britain, most people still wanted to hear the familiar singles. Unfortunately by the end of 1968, the Floyd were feeling thoroughly alienated by provincial audiences, as Roger told John Salisbury when asked if the band knew when they had played badly: "It's a bad feeling. We're aware of it. We don't just think "Well fuck them, bloody teach them a lesson"... There are some occasions though if there's a crowd, say in the Starlight Ballroom, Greenford, and they expect us to give them 'Knock On Wood' followed by 'Ride Your Pony' and 'In The Midnight Hour,' we tend to think it doesn't matter whether we play badly or not. If we had the choice we wouldn't play, for instance, the Top Rank or Mecca ballrooms, or anywhere with a revolving stage, but we played them a few times in the past, and they've all made quite sure they'll never see us again. Universities are nice; we don't immediately think 'I wonder if they'll throw bottles here?'."

The university circuit was only just beginning to get established and though the Floyd depended heavily on this market in the early Seventies, it was not yet big enough to sustain them. But even with a sympathetic audience of college students or hippies, they still needed to evolve an act that didn't involve an attempt to play their material in the same way it appeared on albums. The light show had provided an added attraction

*O'Rourke was to remain Pink Floyd's manager until his death in 2003.

in the early days, but travelling with a light show was very problematic and the equipment often got broken in the back of the van. These were the days before aluminium flight cases and roll-on, roll off containers; even the clever idea of putting wheels on heavy speaker cabinets had not yet occurred to rock and roll road crews, they were still physically lifting them around.

Roger, speaking in December 1968: "The emphasis is now on the sound because we can't be bothered to fuck about with lights any more; until we've got enough bread to get them together and a stable place." The plan was to find a large hall and be given a number of days "with no one else allowed near it" to prepare their show. The idea the Floyd had was to become the blueprint for all their future shows.

Roger: "We're going to do something in darkness. Basically it's a work, I suppose, not a play or a series of pop songs. It'll probably last for an hour and a half to two hours, with an interval in the middle, because 40 live minutes or an hour is about as long as anyone can really be involved in anything. The audience will sit within a ring of about eight speakers, and the basis of the whole thing will be on tape. We'll be working live on our instruments and doing other things as well, and then there'll probably be dancers. The whole thing is built around this machine we've had made called a spacial co-ordinator; it can direct or focus the sound wherever we want it inside the circle."

It was Pink Floyd's version of Andy Warhol's Exploding Plastic Inevitable crossed with the Who's pop opera; the idea of spectacle, a Pink Floyd experience, separate, and in addition to their recorded output.

MORE

The nature of Pink Floyd's music made it suitable for film soundtracks; something they were keen to try out. Their first celluloid venture had been *San Francisco*, a fast moving 15 minute short made by Anthony Stern, the soundtrack a unique 1966 studio version of 'Interstellar Overdrive'. This was followed by Peter Whitehead's unreleased 1967 Swinging London study *Tonite Let's All Make Love in London* (see Chapter 7) whose opening titles featured a three minute edit of the 'Interstellar Overdrive' version that Whitehead recorded at Sound Techniques.* In late 1967 the Floyd were invited to supply the music for Peter Sykes' *The Committee* (released in 1968). I went to an advance screening a few weeks before it was premiered at the Cameo Poly on September 26. The film starred ex-Manfred Mann singer Paul Jones, who was very enthusiastic about both the film and the music at the screening. The undoubted highlight of the film was a party scene with Arthur Brown in full 'I am the God of Hell Fire' mode.

The Floyd, who don't appear on screen, seem to have been not quite so keen on the film. In *Inside Out*, Nick Mason states that the whole soundtrack was made in a single morning "and was not very convincing". My own memory is that it was quite enjoyable, but that the film suffered from being in rather grey black and white.*

The band was then approached by Barbet Schroeder. Nick: "Barbet Schroeder's proposal, which had taken an interesting subject, was very attractive. Besides that, it was an exciting exercise, because Barbet Schroeder is a director who is really easy to work with." There was also the added attraction of £600 each which was clearly a more attractive proposition than a week of gigs scattered all across Britain during a cold January. It was Schroeder's first film as a director – he had previously produced five films by Eric Rohmer and one by Claude Chabrol so it was a new departure for him.

Rick: "His feeling about music for movies was, in those days, that he didn't want a soundtrack to go behind the movie. All he wanted was, literally, if the radio was switched on in the car, for example, he wanted something to come out of the car. Or someone goes and switches the TV on, or whatever it is. He wanted the soundtrack to relate exactly to what was happening in the movie, rather than a film score backing the visuals." This was something of a breakthrough at the time, especially the scene where the music stops and the camera shows that the tape has stopped running. Barbet Schroeder: "That was to really show that the music was not coming out of thin air, but was really the music that the people in the movie were listening to."

At the end of January 1969, the band established themselves at Pye studios in Marble Arch, and working very fast, completed the soundtrack in eight days, working from midnight to 8 am, laying down 16 tracks in just five sessions. Rick, Nick and David wrote the music, Roger would go into another room and write the lyrics, then they would all work out how to fit the two together; it was like a factory assembly line.

Once they had the song, the band recorded it on the spot. Barbet Schroeder: "It was very hard work, and the people in the studio didn't know the Pink Floyd, and would say 'Who are these people that work so hard?' They were really working harder than other people. Then we watched the movie to double check."

David: "Yes, it was eight days to do everything from writing, recording, editing… but everything we did was accepted by the director. He never asked us to redo anything."

Nick: "We were very pleased with our music… it was, in our mind, a succession of songs. It wasn't a Pink Floyd album, but a group of songs. But still, the whole was balanced, with different rhythms and tempos. I agree when it's said it didn't have the strength of *Dark Side Of The Moon* or *Meddle*. However, it was a great success and became, most of all in France, a disco classic."

Barbet Schroeder: "My movie wouldn't have been as famous without Pink Floyd music! The public wanted a movie about those times… I made the movie because it was the right thing to do at the time. Pink Floyd were making the music that was best adapted to the movie at the time – spacey and very in tune with nature. For me it was a movie about love and destruction, where drugs were playing a very important part. It was not like a sign of the times, it was more like a German romantic movie or *L'Ange Bleu* by Steril Misengil. In America the movie didn't do well at all because the dialogue was not tailored to young Americans. There was no hippie slang in the dialogue. They were speaking a completely different language at the time. But it was very big in Europe."

On CD the music shows the haste with which it was composed and recorded. The playing is often uneven, particularly Nick's drum rolls on 'The Nile Song', and in Rick's Cecil Taylor imitations on 'Up The Khyber', though it was obviously fun to play it could have been better realised and more original. But it is a pleasant album and, more importantly, in terms of the band's career, it made them famous in Europe.

The art school rock ideal, as identified by Simon Frith, was to express an individual vision of the world using every technological resource available to them and yet not be corrupted by the commercial forces brought to bear on them by the record companies. There was a clear difference between rock and pop: pop was hopelessly compromised by the fact that both its form and content were determined by market forces whereas rock used the mass media forms but was – ideally – not corrupted by them. Enough people were interested in supporting artistic endeavour to support the group and, in the case of the Floyd, to make them very wealthy.

It was the birth of 'progressive rock', supported by a new, artistic, audience described by Frith who wrote: 'The Floyd's fans were equally determined to be different from ordinary pop people and they realised this through superior *consumption*.' Pink Floyd were *the* progressive rock band, and as the university circuit developed, they appealed very much to this more cerebral audience. There was a slight problem in that progressive rock relied on a higher than usual competence in musicianship. Nick sometimes seemed uncomfortable playing outside his usual tempo and, because he invariably played behind the beat, his style was not well suited to any more funky rock 'n' roll passages. Roger's interest lay almost entirely in the overall form and the lyrics; musically he was only a barely adequate bass player.

"He had developed his own limited, or very simple style," said David in describing Roger's playing. "He was never very keen on improving himself as a bass player and half the time I would play bass on the records because I would tend to do it quicker. Right back to those early records; I mean, at least half the bass on all recorded output is me anyway… I think it's been said [before], but it's certainly not something we go around advertising. Rog used to come in and say, 'Thank you very much' to me once in a while for winning him bass playing polls."

Gilmour himself had problems during his early days with the group: "I didn't know what the hell I was trying to play at the time to be quite honest. I'd really no idea. What I was used to playing, the style I had, didn't fit Pink Floyd at the time, and I didn't really know quite what to do. Gradually over the years my style changed to fit Pink Floyd, and Pink Floyd changed to fit my style." David added melody and a sense of harmony to the music and brought it slightly more into the mainstream.

In his own playing he brought a singing tone – richer than Clapton's, statelier than Beck's – that virtually defines the progressive rock of the period. Unable to play fast, he never attempted to compete with the speedy guitar virtuosos who pulled grimaces as they attempted to play those ever so difficult high notes, nor did he resort to playing with a bow or a double necked guitar: his soaring solos were like sheets of sound,

∗Though the Floyd appeared on screen for less than a minute all of Whitehead's footage can now be seen in *Pink Floyd 1966/67*.
∗*The Committee* has recently been issued privately on DVD.

sonic sculptures, or what Zappa liked to call "air sculptures". They added to the architectural quality already there in the band and contributed greatly to its new direction, away from Syd's jerky improvisations, into huge, formally-planned sound constructions.

The next significant event was 'The Massed Gadgets of Auximenes: More Furious Madness from the Pink Floyd' concert at the Royal Festival Hall in London on April 14, 1969. The show was in two parts with a 15 minute interval. The first act was a performance of 'The Man', an evocation of a day in the life of the average wage slave, inspired by a huge piece of translated graffiti, originating from Paris in 1968, that ran for hundreds of feet along the walls of the Metropolitan line train track near Paddington station. Roger saw it each time he came into town from the small flat he and Judy shared in Pennard Mansions at the eastern end of the Goldhawk Road. The words read: 'Get up, go to work, come home, go to bed, get up, go to work, come home, go to bed, get up, go to work, come home, go to bed, get up, go to work, come home, go to bed. How much longer can you keep it up? How much longer before you crack?'

Waters told John Harris: "It was inspired... it was on this wall and it seemed to go on forever, and as the train sped up it would go quicker and quicker until – bang! You suddenly went into a tunnel." 'The Man' began with a daybreak sequence – in this case 'Grantchester Meadows', something the Floyd were very good at – followed by work and a tea break. The band built a table on stage with much rhythmic hammering and sawing and when it was done, the roadies came in with a pot of tea and switched on a transistor radio and put a microphone in front of it so that the audience could hear whatever happened to be being broadcast at that time while the band sat drinking their tea. The audience loved this bit. The piece continued with nightfall, a sex sequence – Nick Mason's 'Doing It' – and finally sleep with a nightmare, here represented by the track 'Cymbaline'. The second and final act consisted of 'The Journey' in which the band visited 'The Pink Jungle', usually known as 'Pow R, Toc H' and 'The Narrow Way'. 'The Journey' featured a silver sea monster – a creature from the deep, representing the nightmare – that lumbered up the aisle, pausing to tap some startled members of the audience on the shoulder, before clambering onstage, examining the flowers arranged along the footlights, and finally disappearing backstage.

The next day Nick reported: "I was surprised how popular the concert was. We had no idea that it would be sold out so quickly. We thought of doing a second concert like the Cream* but that means four hours playing in one evening and in the first show one is bound to hold something back, simply to conserve energy, and in the second, one is inevitably tired, so that neither is very satisfactory. Basically I was pleased with last night's show; it was definitely a very important step for us as a group. I remember our show two years ago at Queen Elizabeth Hall when we demonstrated our first 'fantastic' sound system and we all thought it was exactly what we wanted to do. But things change, and this concert was just as vital as that one was, and since then a lot of ideas have changed about the kind of music we want to play... If we can develop this kind of thing into an even bigger and better stage without getting too technically involved, we will be going in the right direction." Nick had been concerned that the famed Azimuth Co-ordinator system was overly elaborate and might have worked better with just four speakers around the hall instead of six to give the illusion of surround-sound. He was however, very pleased with the stereo footsteps sequence.

In general it was usually Nick and Roger who enjoyed this type of presentation, the sound effects, the showmanship side of performance, whereas Rick and David were more concerned with purely musical issues. Between them they had a nice balance. As far as the audience was concerned, they had come up with a winning formula for a stage show.

UMMAGUMMA

Work on the third Pink Floyd album proper began early in the year and the LP was originally slated for release in March. The group had a number of disparate ideas for their own work but, recognising that none of them was yet ready for a solo album, they opted, at Rick Wright's suggestion, to each produce half a side; Rick's interest had always been more in the direction of modern classical composition and free jazz and he was feeling dissatisfied with his contribution to the group's music. When the band agreed to his idea he threw himself into it and had finished his contribution 'Sysyphus'* by January 25, telling *Record Mirror*: "There are no electronic sounds,

Below:
Ummagumma
was released in
October, 1969.

no juggling with tapes. Theoretically you could do it live, and the only reason I did virtually all of it myself is that it was quicker that way. I didn't write out scores, I drew graphs."

Roger was reported as still working on his but David's was "still in the ideas stage". He found it very difficult to compose an extended piece, particularly the lyrics and when David called Roger for help he was turned down flat. Gilmour clearly never rated his offering, 'The Narrow Way', and in 1983 he more or less disowned it: "We'd decided to make the damn album and each of us to do a piece of music on our own... It was just desperation really, trying to think of something to do, to write by myself. I'd never written anything before, I just went into a studio and started waffling about, tacking bits and pieces together."

Nick enrolled his wife Lindy, an accomplished flautist, to help him with 'The Grand Vizier's Garden Party', and progressed so quickly that he taped his sections over twice before the others were finished.

Roger's 'Grantchester Meadows' with its sparing, but enormously effective use of field recordings of birds, swans taking off and even a dog fox barking, is the only one of the four that really holds up. The barely discernable voices of children playing in the meadows and the final, clever, stereo trick of a bee or wasp being swatted was particularly well executed and people at the time loved to use it to show off their new stereo hi-fi's. Roger's other track 'Several Species Of Small Furry Animals Gathered Together In A Cave And Grooving With A Pict' was an audio experiment, something described by him as, "A bit of concrete poetry. Those were sounds that I made, the voice and the hand slapping were all human generated – no musical instruments." When the Canadian interviewer suggested that the track was designed to "get into someone's head" Roger took up the idea: "And just push him about a bit, nothing deliberate, not a deliberate blow on the nose, just to sort of mess him around a bit."

The group agreed beforehand that they would not play their contributions to each other until each member had finished. The idea was that they would just come in with a finished product. Roger told Caroline Boucher, "It would have been a better album if we'd gone away, done the things, come back together and discussed them, and people could have come in and made comments. I don't think it's good to work in total isolation." However, by the time they had finished recording the band had used up all their allotted studio time so it was not possible.

EMI were disturbed to be presented with *Ummagumma**and gave the band a hard time about releasing it. Roger: "That was the final time when we realised that they didn't know anything, cause they didn't believe in *Ummagumma*. They didn't believe it would sell at all. And it came out [in October '69] and sold better, far better than anyone thought." Because of the record's ambitious, experimental nature, EMI decided to move the Floyd over from Columbia to the company's progressive/underground imprint Harvest, launched in July and set up by their man in the know, Malcolm Jones, with assistance from none other than Peter Jenner and Andrew King.

The decision to pair the studio disc with a live album was largely because the band's management thought punters would feel ripped off to find four mini solo albums, not a bona fide Pink Floyd effort. It was also issued at a budget-friendly price. The live set, recorded at Manchester University and Birmingham's Mothers Club, comprising 'Astronomy Domine', 'Careful With That Axe Eugene', 'Set The Controls For The Heart Of The Sun' and 'A Saucerful Of Secrets' more than made up for any commercial misgivings and, most importantly, it introduced American listeners to the Floyd's live show. 'Astronomy Domine' probably kept their erstwhile leader Syd Barrett going for a year or two in composing royalties. His non-committal comment on the album was: "They've probably done very well. The singing's very good and the drumming is good as well."

THE MADCAP LAUGHS

Syd sometimes still turned up to gigs where it had to be explained that he could not join his former bandmates on stage. He was taking less acid but had increased his intake of Mandrax which made him sloppy. In January 1969, he and his friend, the painter Duggie Fields, moved into 29 Wetherby Mansions, Earls Court Square in south west London. Syd threw a mattress on the floor in the corner, unrolled a dirty carpet, stacked his art school paintings in the corner and hung a wire-and-paper construction from the ceiling. He wired up the hi-fi, also on the floor and leaned his album collection against the wall next to his guitar.

*Cream's played two 'farewell' concerts at the Royal Albert Hall in November '68.
*More commonly spelt as 'Sisyphus' based on the character from Greek mythology who was condemned to forever push a boulder up a steep hill only for it to roll back down again.
*There is still some controversy over the word *Ummagumma*, though it is generally thought to be Cambridge slang for sex.

Above: Syd's first solo album, The Madcap Laughs, was released in January, 1970.

Apart from these, Barrett brought with him his few possessions – several books, including the *I-Ching* and some clothes. He decided to paint the floorboards alternately orange and blue but did not bother to clean them first. Cigarette ends, dog and cat hair, dust, all were mixed in with the paint. Legend has it that he also, literally, painted himself into a corner but as he presumably did one colour at a time that seems apocryphal. He stretched brown Hessian over the windows so that they could be opened. Duggie Fields complained: "There was a stench in the room that was unbearable. As soon as he went out, I'd take advantage of the occasion to clean up, but he hardly ever went out."

That was not entirely true because in April (and continuing over the summer) at EMI Studios, Syd commenced recording, albeit with some difficulty, the tracks for *The Madcap Laughs*. That March, Malcolm Jones, at Harvest, received a message from the bookings department to say that Syd had called to ask if he could have studio time to record again. He was still under contract and claimed to have lots of new material. On the phone at least he sounded very together and he acted in a professional way when returning to Abbey Road.

Barrett had recorded a few tracks with Peter Jenner the previous year but they were incomplete and unusable. The first order of business was to play them through and see if anything could be salvaged. The tracks were brought up from the vault and on April 10, Syd overdubbed vocals and guitar onto two tracks: 'Swan Lee' and 'Clowns And Jugglers' and though neither was released until the *Opel* album of Barrett outtakes in 1988 it was a promising start.

The next day was even better. In his book *The Making Of Madcap Laughs* Jones wrote: "The next evening we got down to business proper. Syd was in a great mood and in fine form, a stark contrast to the rumours and stories I'd been fed with. In a little over five hours we laid down vocal and guitar tracks (extra backings on most came later) for four new songs and two old." Jones recorded nine takes of 'Opel' and got a 'best' version. Here the producer went against normal studio practice and instead of laying down backing tracks first and overdubbing vocals and guitar, Jones captured Syd's guitar and vocals first – which in any case changed with each take – knowing he could always overdub a rhythm section on later. Next was the uptempo 'Love You', resulting in three complete takes to choose from, followed by a new composition 'It's No Good Trying' resulting in two usable takes, and 'Terrapin', one of Barrett's most well-known songs, recorded in a single pass plus an overdubbed guitar and extra vocal line.

As they were doing so well, Jones played through two more incomplete 1968 recordings from the vaults. Syd overdubbed guitar and vocal onto 'Late Night', and added double-tracked vocals to 'Golden Hair', his setting of the Joyce poem. Jones was overjoyed. The previous year Syd had wasted time in the studio, broke microphones and was generally unmanageable. Now in just two days they had eight tracks completed. The third and final day of this booking, Syd brought in Jerry Shirley on drums and Joker's Wild/Flowers bassist John 'Willie' Wilson and laid down two more tracks using an amp they stopped off and borrowed from David Gilmour on the way to Abbey Road.

Something of the old Syd returned a week later, however, when the entire session was spent trying to overdub various noises that he had recorded while riding pillion on the back of a friend's motorcycle onto a 20 minute long abandoned 1968 track called 'Rhamadan'. Syd's tape was unusable, nor could they approximate it with motorcycle sounds from EMI's sound effects library, but a good start to the *Madcap* recording sessions had been made. Syd returned on April 28 and supervised the transfer of the master tracks from four-track to eight-track. Malcolm Jones was away sick so Syd did it himself, using the opportunity to overdub a few little extras onto 'Love You'.

A week or so later Syd was back in Studio 3, this time accompanied by Robert Wyatt on drums, Mike Ratledge on keyboards and Hugh Hopper on bass; otherwise known as the Soft Machine. They had been playing a gig at the 100 Club on Oxford Street and Syd had gone to see them. Afterwards, as the group were waiting in the street for a cab, Syd came up to them and started chatting. Hugh Hopper: "In his very, very oblique way he said, 'Would you like to come along and record?' He had most of the tracks just put down, the guitar and voice. He just said, 'I'd like you to play on these two tracks and do what you can.' He didn't even tell us how it went, we just had to listen to it until we had some idea. His music is not very symmetrical, you really have to listen and then it changes suddenly."

Robert Wyatt: "I thought they were rehearsals! We'd say, 'What key is it in, Syd?'

and he'd say 'Yeah.' Or, 'That's funny Syd, there's a bar of two and a half beats and then it seems to slow up and then there's five beats there' and he'd go, 'Oh really?' And we just sat there with the tape running, trying to work it out when he stood up and said, 'Right, thank you very much.'"

Wyatt and co. each received the standard £8 session fee and left, rather bemused. They appear on 'Love You', ''It's No Good Trying' and 'Clowns And Jugglers' (later retitled 'Octopus')

Hugh Hopper: "I enjoyed playing on them because they were interesting tracks and I think we made them even more interesting with what we did to them."

Syd had been seeing a lot of David Gilmour, any residual animosity about being replaced presumably having been resolved, and he even visited Gilmour backstage at a Floyd gig. David, for his part, was taking a keen interest in what Syd was doing. It was not long before the idea came up that Gilmour might produce a track or two with Barrett in addition to the sessions with Malcolm Jones. In fact, David, later joined by Roger Waters for the final session, now took over the production.

Malcolm Jones: "At the time I never felt any sense of being ousted from my role as producer. I had fared pretty well, and I still feel that there was enough already made to complete an album. . . My original ambition had been fulfilled – to get Syd back on record. How it was done was of no objection to me as long as it was done professionally, so when Dave came to me and said that Syd wanted him and Roger to do the remaining parts of the album, I acquiesced."

Though Syd was in a hurry to get his record out, Pink Floyd were busy completing *Ummagumma* which prevented Gilmour and Waters from devoting much of their time to his project. The remaining tracks on the album were recorded on June 12 and 13 and a final session on July 26, after the Floyd returned from a long tour of Holland. There were a number of delays, largely caused by the Floyd's schedule, and their summer holidays, which meant that the mixing wasn't done until August and the final running order established in September. Syd's first solo album, *The Madcap Laughs*, was finally released on January 2, 1970.

Below: Syd Barrett pictured at home in his Earl's Court Square flat with Eskimo girlfriend Iggy – an out-take from the sleeve shot for The Madcap Laughs.

CHAPTER ELEVEN
ATOM HEART MOTHER TO MEDDLE

CHAPTER ELEVEN
ATOM HEART
MOTHER
TO MEDDLE

ZABRISKIE POINT

According to David Gilmour, Pink Floyd were keen to get into high profile film scores – the reason they wrote the music for *More* – so they were delighted when Michelangelo Antonioni approached them to compose the soundtrack of *Zabriskie Point*, a sprawling but beautifully filmed collage of images of the American hippie and anti-war movement. Antonioni had first seen Pink Floyd at the *IT* launch party at the Roundhouse in 1966 but it was hearing 'Careful With That Axe, Eugene' that made him send them plane tickets to Rome.

Recording the soundtrack took two weeks, spread over November and early December, 1969, with at least two trips back to Britain to fulfil already contracted gigs. Because of the short notice, it had only been possible to book a studio from midnight until nine in the morning. The band were put up at the luxurious Hotel Massimo D'Azeglio near the Termini Station where they were on a fixed rate which included a $40 a day food allowance to be spent at the hotel's famous turn-of-the-century restaurant; an enormous amount of money. It did not take them long to realise that the allowance was wasted if they did not order the very best on offer.

Roger: "Every day we would get up at about 4.30 in the afternoon. We'd pop into the bar and sit there until about 7.00 then we'd stagger into the restaurant where we'd eat for about two hours and drink. By about half way through the two weeks, the bloke there was beginning to suss out what we wanted; we kept asking for these ridiculous wines so by the end he was coming up with these really insane wines."

Nick: "The peach melba was good too. I used to start with sole bonne femme followed by the roast leg of lamb cooked with rosemary. Then a peach melba or a crepe suzette, or perhaps both."

The studio was only a short walk away, down the Via Cavour, where the group would exchange pleasantries with the hookers who worked there. Roger: "We could have finished the whole thing in about five days because there wasn't too much to do. Antonioni was there and we did some great stuff, but he'd listen and go – and I remember he had this terrible twitch – 'Eet's very beauteeful but eet's too sad' or 'Eet's too strong.' It was always something that stopped it being perfect. You'd change whatever was wrong and he'd still be unhappy. It was hell, sheer hell." The band worked until eight in the morning, returned to the hotel for breakfast, then slept.

Rick: "It's all improvised, but nonetheless it was really hard work. We had each piece of music and we did, say, six takes of each, and he'd choose the best. Antonioni's not hard to work with – but he's a perfectionist... every night for two weeks to get twenty minutes of music, it was hard, but it was worth it."

In the end Antonioni felt he needed a more American sounding score and only used

three of the tracks:* 'Heart Beat, Pig Meat,' 'Crumbling Land,' and 'Come In Number 51, Your Time Is Up,' an improvised remake of 'Careful With That Axe,' which was utilised very effectively over the multiple slow motion shots of a luxury desert home exploding. The Floyd were understandably irritated when Antonioni flew the Grateful Dead to Italy to provide more music. Roger felt it was because the band's sound was beginning to pervade the whole film: "He was afraid of Pink Floyd becoming part of the film, rather than it staying entirely Antonioni. So we were quite upset when he used all these other things. I mean if he had used things which we found better... there were only two pieces of music in the film that we did, really, and the other piece of music we did, was like, any other group could have done, really. A direct imitation really of Byrds, Crosby, Stills and Nash, or something."

After this relaxing interlude, the Floyd returned to the more rigorous life on the road. Steve O'Rourke certainly pushed them and, though it was an exhausting pace, the band was finally making decent money. Their overdraft was being paid off and each member was earning a decent income. But along with the touring came the need to record yet another album and, as usual, they had very few ideas. Pink Floyd music has always been about illusive atmospheres, textures, changes in timbre, soundscapes; they are not regarded for their catchy melodies or memorable lyrics even though, undoubtedly, there are some. Assembling an album was always a long slow process for the Floyd but the main theme they had for their next LP looked like developing into a long piece, enough to take up the whole of one side.

*Antonioni rejected the lyrical Rick Wright piano piece that later became 'Us And Them' on *Dark Side Of The Moon*.

David came up with the original riff for what became 'Atom Heart Mother' in a rehearsal hall. Roger: "He played that riff... and we all listened to it and thought, 'Oh, that's quite nice...' but we all thought the same thing which was that it sounds like a theme from some awful Western; it had that kind of... slight pastiche, heroic, plodding quality to it... of horses silhouetted against the sunset. Which is why we thought it'd be a good idea to play on that really and cover it in horns and strings and voices and whatever else. So that's why we did it; because it sounded like a... very heavy movie score. I think we found... I have no idea why we fouled it up. I think we probably did it because we were... we felt rather inadequate to cope with it."

Keeping to the cinematic sound, each member contributed to David's original theme, adding and taking away parts until they had a long piece that they were satisfied with. Using the working title that accurately described its construction, 'The Amazing Pudding', they premiered it live at the Theatre des Champs Elysées in Paris on January 23, 1970.

In March they toured Europe, playing five cities in Germany before going on to Sweden, Denmark and France. This was a year of festivals including the Bath Festival of Blues and Progressive Music, the Isle of Wight Festival – where they contributed to the PA for the whole event and David Gilmour mixed Jimi Hendrix's sound – the Great Medicine Ball in Canterbury, the Holland Pop Festival in Rotterdam, the First Open Air Pop Festival at Aachen in Germany, and a whole group of festivals in the South of France: the XI Festival International de Jazz in Antibes, the Festival d'Aix-en-Provence, the Festival Maudit de Biot, Popanalia in Nice, the St. Tropez Music Festival and the Fête de St Raphaël.

In Britain they premiered their new piece, now called 'Atom Heart Mother', at Blackhill's Garden Party, a free concert held in Hyde Park on July 18 organised by their ex-managers. They used a brass ensemble and a choir and, according to *Disc and Music Echo*, "gave an hour of beautifully mature music, soothing and inspiring to listen to."

ATOM HEART MOTHER

Whenever they could the band squeezed recording dates between gigs: after a couple of weeks in March and a week in April they had the 25 minute title track blocked out, but not all the time signatures were the same and a beat was missing here and there from the edits. Though the pieces sounded great on stage, the band recognised that it was really a bit dull and in need of some colour. As none of them could write music well enough to properly arrange the piece they approached Ron Geesin to fix it. Nick Mason knew Geesin through a mutual friend, Sam Cutler, as they lived near to each other in Notting Hill.

Ron had been approached to compose the soundtrack (released on Harvest) for a documentary called *The Body*, directed by Tony Garnett. It was a film of a journey through the body itself using micro-photography that was originally intended to have no words, just music as its soundtrack. Ron: "It was great – it told its own story of travelling through the human body, but then they were forced to get Vanessa Redgrave and someone else to narrate. They did all sorts of pansy stuff over the top of it."

Roger Waters was brought in to add some lyrics to the music, urgently required by the distributor, resulting in the whole of Pink Floyd playing on the closing track, 'Give Birth To A Smile'. Roger's recordings took place between January and March 1970 at Geesin's Ladbroke Grove studio and during that time they became good friends and even golf partners, so when the Floyd needed an arranger for 'Atom Heart Mother', Ron was the first person they thought of. In April, with EMI pressuring them for an album, they handed the tapes over to Geesin, asking him to write melodies and arrangements for choir and a horn section to liven up the less interesting bits.

The band then left for their third American tour, taking along their Azimuth Co-ordinator. In New York, Bill Graham had only offered them a 40 minute slot at the Fillmore East on a bill with three other groups so they rented the venue from him themselves and sold it out. They also took with them their own 4000 watt PA sound system because they didn't like the Fillmore's acoustics; Graham had put very little money into the place, which was the old Village Theatre, and there were no acoustic baffles on the high ceiling to absorb the sound. With their live show now showcasing 'Atom Heart Mother', and the record company agreeing to subsidise a horn section and a choir for the New York and Los Angeles segments of the tour, the band was particularly anxious that the sound be good. They had not been looking forward to the trip.

Above: Atom Heart Mother was released in October, 1970.

Rick: "I don't like living in hotels for weeks and there is a lot of violence in America." The Floyd now had several years of experience of being on the road, and the groupies and room service food no longer held the same romantic appeal. Their concerns were justified because the band almost missed the last date of the tour when all their equipment – the PA system including 12 speakers, Rick's electric organ, two drum kits and four guitars – was stolen in New Orleans. Roger: "That was nearly a total disaster. We sat down in our hotel thinking, 'Well that's it, it's all over.' We were pouring out our troubles to a girl who worked at the hotel and she said her father worked for the FBI. The police hadn't helped us much, but the FBI got to work, and four hours later it was found. £15,000 worth."

Back in England, Ron Geesin was sweating over the *Atom Heart Mother* tapes at Abbey Road. Ron: "I think that they had hit creative exhaustion. They had been battling away with each other and had not learnt the skills of pulling off, retreating from each other, and I think they were rather heavily battling. I think they were creatively exhausted and they needed the influence of an outside view... so as I was their mate at the time, they proposed this thing that they wanted brass and choir on, this long piece, and they provided me with really what I would call the backing tracks, probably they were a bit more than backing tracks – they did have the sound that was the astral slide guitar on them in places."

Geesin wrote a score for a 10-piece brass section and a 20 voice choir, plus one solo cello. Unfortunately the EMI studio session mafia did not like to play anything difficult, and made his life as difficult as possible by continually asking unnecessary questions and playing badly. Eventually an agreement was worked out after Ron suggested that he and one of the recalcitrant brass players go outside and settle their differences man to man, and the session men plodded their way through the score. Matters were not helped by the fact that it was a sweateringly hot May, and the backing tapes were not all in the same time signature, having been poorly edited together. Geesin quickly got himself into a desperate state but was rescued by choirmaster John Aldiss who saw how obdurate the session men were being. In June, Aldiss took over as conductor and managed to get a useable recording out of them with Ron advising from the sidelines. But Geesin was not satisfied. He regarded the recording as "a bloody disaster". Ron: "I turned to Steve O'Rourke and said, 'That's a good rehearsal, can we do it again?'"

Though Geesin is on a one fifth royalty for what became one whole side of the album, and some of his arrangements, like the solo cello, contributed greatly to the album's success, the band did not list his name among the credits. This was something his wife was particularly incensed by, but Ron was more circumspect, having worked in the music business for years and knowing how musicians behave. He was bitterly disappointed at how it turned out, mostly because in order to compensate for the fact that Nick Mason plays behind the beat, the orchestral parts were all played exactly one beat late, ruining his arrangement.

Geesin told Nick Schaffner: "It turned out that from Nicky's point of view, beat number one was one beat off that – and he insisted that everything I'd written for that section had to be moved one beat. So that whole part has all my writing one beat away from where it should have been. I should have just rubbed out all the bar lines and moved them one beat up, but I wasn't clever enough." When learning this, it becomes immediately apparent and the horns in particular seem to drag unbearably.*

The album went to number one in Britain, thanks largely to Ron's work on the title track: "I took the backing tracks and formed all the top, all the... I don't know, icing on the cake... working, most of the time on my own, but part of the choir section was done with Rick. Say the first half of it was done in collaboration with him, but I did all the writing. It was really just him and I discussing where the float should go, where the wisps of smoke and lines ought to go."

On July 16, two days before the Hyde Park concert, the Floyd were recording a version of the track – still known as 'The Amazing Pudding' – for a John Peel *In Concert* programme at the BBC Paris Cinema on Lower Regent Street. As they were relaxing outside a pub at 7pm on a sunny evening, enjoying a break from recording, BBC producer Jeff Griffin asked what it was going to be called as forms had to be filled in for collecting performance royalties. They still didn't have a proper name for the piece. Peel walked down the street and bought a copy of the *Evening Standard* and, looking through the headlines, seeking inspiration, they came upon a small story about a woman that had an atom powered pacemaker fitted in her chest. The headline was 'Atom Heart Mother'. "Oh, yes," said Roger, "that's a nice name, we'll call it that!"

*When Geesin saw the Floyd perform 'Atom Heart Mother' at Blackhill's Garden Party he was so frustrated that he left in tears before the end.

Rick was never very happy about the album recording but said, "I did enjoy playing it live when it worked, particularly in America, where for some reason musicians just got into the thing a lot more. I don't know why. I certainly enjoyed playing it live 'cause it was a totally new experience of working with other people. The actual recording of it is not that good."

Roger had stronger opinions: "*Atom Heart Mother* is a really awful and embarrassing record. But most of the albums were good in one way or another. I honestly believe we were very progressive for the time." He thought it was a good thing to have attempted but didn't think they brought it off successfully. "People accuse us of being pretentious, but if you don't push the boundaries, if you don't verge on the borders of being pretentious, I don't think you advance an awful lot. You've got to have courage and not care what people think about you at that moment."

The sleeve was the first truly striking Hipgnosis production for Pink Floyd; a very conscious attempt to get away from the obvious psychedelic designs that other progressive rock groups used. Storm Thorgerson: "The idea came from a friend of mine in conversation. He just said, 'How about a picture of a cow?' as an example of something pretty damn ordinary, and immediately he said it, I kind of twigged and went out and shot a cow, and I took a picture like how I remembered at school, in an animal textbook – it's supposed to be the ultimate picture of a cow – it's just totally cow... it should say 'COW' to you."

Sadly the photo of Lulubelle, the pedigree Friesian, was not taken in Grantchester Meadows and so therefore does not support my 'Pink Floyd-as-a-Cambridge-band' theme; it was shot outside Potters Bar in Hertfordshire. It was a brilliant choice and oddly, it suited the Floyd whereas it would have looked merely absurd on a Yes or Emerson, Lake & Palmer sleeve. Somehow it corresponded to the stately, processional, anthemic theme of 'Atom Heart Mother,' evoking some notion of a timeless England.[*]

Pretentious or not, *Atom Heart Mother* was tuned in to the Zeitgeist of that moment: the tiredness after all the late nights and drugs of the Sixties, the more introspective reflection on life as that generation grew up, established more permanent relationships, started families, decided how to live in the new world they had made. It also included Roger Waters' best lyrics to date, the intimate self-analysis of 'If'. Rick's candid confessional 'Summer 68' was equally revelatory, the lyrics describing his mixed feelings about a groupie encountered on the road combined with some of his more confident piano playing and a rock arrangement equal to the singer-songwriter work emanating from Laurel Canyon at the time.

The singer-songwriter tradition was continued in David's 'Fat Old Sun' which owed more than a nod towards the Kinks' 'Lazy Old Sun', from their 1967 LP *Something Else* – as he said later, 'They've never sued me'. The solo in 'Fat Old Sun' also shared similarities with Eric Clapton's 'Layla' – recorded and released at the same time – with Gilmour's beautiful long solo with its high tracking harmony, like grace notes, buried low in the mix. The church bells and countryside sound effects came from the Abbey Road tape library but are a definite reference to David's upbringing on Grantchester Meadows. Though the band were later very critical of 'Alan's Psychedelic Breakfast' with its stereo recording of their roadie, Alan Stiles, frying eggs, the public enjoyed

'Atom Heart M
awful and emb
But most of the
good in one wa
I honestly belie
very progressiv

Roger Waters

*The sleeve also looked terrific on the huge billboards on Sunset Strip when the album was released in October 1970.
*The *Barrett* sessions ran February, April, June and July, 1970.

the result and it was possibly this touch of levity that just tipped sales of the album to enable it to reach number one (in the UK; number 55 in the US).

BARRETT

Simultaneous with recording *Atom Heart Mother*, David had been at work producing Syd's second solo album at EMI Studios. He had decided to try and unite the tracks by using the same session men throughout and brought back Jerry Shirley, who was now drumming in Humble Pie, and Rick Wright on keyboards. David played virtually everything else, as needed. Peter Bown was to be the balance engineer at Abbey Road but he had not worked with Syd since 1968 and was a little surprised when David warned him: "Are you prepared to do this Peter, because it's going to be pretty heavy" The tape operator was Alan Parsons who was also concurrently working on *Atom Heart Mother*.

The first session was on February 26, 1970* when 'Baby Lemonade' was cut in just one take (though there were later overdubs). This was an encouraging start as they also recorded 'Maisie' that same day. But Syd was in bad shape for most of the sessions. He had no studio discipline and Bown had to hit record and then stand near Barrett in the studio with a microphone in each hand trying to keep him within six foot range because Syd would wander away from any fixed mikes. The next day 'Gigolo Aunt' and decent demo vocal tracks of four other songs were laid down. Syd had a habit of stopping after a few bars and it was a major battle trying to get him to sing all the way through a take, but if he was encouraged to continue by the musicians carrying on playing he would sometimes pick up where he left off. By transferring all the vocal tracks to multi-track tape, they were able to jump from one track to another and assemble complete vocals but it was a laborious task.

David: "Trying to find a technique of working with Syd was so difficult. You had to pre-record tracks without him, working from one version of the song he had done, and then sit Syd down afterwards and try to get him to play and sing along, with a lot of dropping in. Or you could do it the other way around, where you'd get him to do a performance of it on his own and then try to dub everything else on top of it. The concept of him performing with another bunch of musicians was clearly impossible because he'd change the song every time. He'd never do a song the same twice. I think quite deliberately."

Barrett trusted Gilmour and would often not communicate to anyone else. He would whisper what he wanted and David would then tell the engineer or musicians what was required. Some days he was so out of it that he even had to be escorted to the toilets. Though Gilmour did eventually construct an album by playing codas and bridges and cleverly looping fragments to extend tracks, there is ultimately an ethical question of whether Syd really knew what was going on. It was rather like Willem de Kooning's last years when he had Alzheimer's and didn't even know who he was. His minders would take him to the studio, show him pictures of his earlier work and give him paints and canvas. He painted pictures, each one worth hundred of thousands of dollars, but many critics felt they were the work of child, not a genuine continuation of the great work that had gone before.

Syd did not approve the final takes and mixes of his songs but he did seem to be

er is a really
ssing record.
ums were
another.
e were
the time.'

aware of how much his friend David was doing for him. Gilmour told *Guitar Heroes*: "I've no idea if they were how he wanted them to be, but as he didn't offer opinions, we had to take it onto ourselves to decide how it should be – which is quite a normal thing with producers – but it wasn't because we were trying to assert that on him, it's just there wasn't anything coming from him to tell us how he thought it should be... The only thing he ever said about it was at the end of the second album, when we'd finished. We were going up the lift in his block of flats in Earls Court, and he turned round to me and he said, 'Thanks – thanks very much.' And that's the only expression of approval or disapproval of anything that I got out of him through two albums I think."

Barrett was released on November 6, 1970 in a sleeve showing insects on the cover, not unlike the ones his father drew in the Botanical Gardens, just up Hill Street, when Syd was a child.

THE DIFFICULT AMERICAN MARKET

Pink Floyd's career seemed to be taking a textbook trajectory; *Atom Heart Mother* was followed by consolidation and strengthening in weak markets. 1971 was marked by a very heavy workload which included a European tour as well as concerts in Japan, Australia and a 26 city tour of the USA and Canada. The band had not yet cracked America where they remained something of an underground sensation. This was partly, if not largely, to do with their record company. The Floyd were switched from Tower to the progressive Harvest counterpart for the release of *Atom Heart Mother* but the corporate culture at Capitol was essentially about hype and money; art, culture, emotion, and commitment didn't really come into it. Tower had done well locally, stocking unorthodox outlets such as the Infinite Mind headshop on Fairfax, and making sure that Lewin's Record Paradise in Hollywood, that specialised in UK imports, were always fully serviced; it was outside LA that the problems arose in marketing.

In Los Angeles it was relatively easy, from their first album onwards Pink Floyd were a cult band and, as rock critic Harvey Kubernik says: "If a girl had those Tower Pink Floyd albums, or brought one to a music/LP party to spin in high school, you usually could make out with them at the invited gathering beyond spin the bottle action... Floyd was the first trance music for many kids in Hollywood. More electronic, spacey, and metallic jazz and not R&B driven and defined. A real eye (and ear) opener."

To help push Pink Floyd up that extra notch a long US tour was planned. They also had to quickly follow up their UK success by recording a new album. Inevitably the band felt the pressure, particularly the stress of two months on the road, every day waiting at a different airport, staying in soulless American hotels and motels. Though hardly the kind of band to destroy hotel rooms and throw TVs into the pool, they did amuse themselves by playing practical jokes on their crew, extra-marital activities and the sort of behaviour that puritan America frowns upon, such as the time when David Gilmour rode a motorcycle through a crowded restaurant in Scottsdale, Arizona.

David: "Funnily enough, it didn't get any reaction at all. People were frightened by it that they all stared very hard at their plates." Though making a point of not going onstage drunk or high, there were plenty of backstage parties afterwards. Roger: 'There was a split. Nick and I were the drinkers. I really didn't start smoking dope until I gave up the fags. I was out of my brains on hash in the early Seventies but I'd given that up by 1975. Floyd was ever really a very druggy band, it was just hash and a bit of acid, except in Syd's case which was tragic because he had a tendency towards schizophrenia and the acid made it infinitely worse."

MEDDLE

Recording sessions for *Meddle* began on January 4, 1971 at Abbey Road. Always conscious of how long it took them to put an album together, the Floyd operated on the principle that any time anyone had a musical idea they would go into the studio and record it, no matter how bizarre.

David: "Some of the ideas we put down were just completely stupid and insane, but we did them just for laughs. We did things like... we'd tell everyone the key and then they'd have to leave the studio while one person would come in and he'd know the key and that's all. He'd play on the same piece of tape without hearing what the other person had played. And we got all of us to do that. *Awful*, absolutely awful! Still, it was jolly good fun anyway." They eventually finished up with 24 separate usable pieces with a working title of 'Nothing, Parts 1-24' and experimented with editing them together in different ways.

The idea was to repeat the successful formula of *Atom Heart Mother* and create one long experimental side and a group of short, more conventional tracks for the other. They got off to a good start with a fortuitous discovery that set the musical tone for the whole of the long piece. The band was in the control room at Abbey Road with the exception of Rick who was in the studio, fooling around with a piano that was miked up through a Lesley amplifier that he had turned up reasonably loud. There was a specific harmonic that always came out louder than any other.

David: "Every time you 'pinged' this one particular note on the piano it came out louder, and that is the 'ping' note on the thing, and then he started playing a little bit and every once in a while he'd hit that note again and we just pottered around a little bit and then we actually put a bit of it down with him actually playing and hitting the note... and that was the start of 'Echoes'."

By using it at the start of the piece it set the tone for what was to come. At first this new long track was called 'The Return Of The Son Of Nothing' and it developed quite quickly once the band had established the atmosphere they were looking for to create a sound poem.

In July they were ready to re-record the whole thing properly, plus the short pieces for the other side, and, as they were no longer contracted to use EMI Studios exclusively, they booked themselves into George Martin's AIR studios on Oxford Street which had a 16-track set-up. It was obvious they had to go elsewhere because if there was ever a group that needed a multi-track facility it was the Floyd who in many ways used the studio itself as an instrument.[*] When they came to record 'Echoes' at AIR, the band found that they couldn't duplicate the particular piano harmonic so they edited the original studio demo onto the master tape.[*]

'Echoes' is pure Floyd: rich, emotional, ethereal and it's easy to see how this led to *Dark Side Of The Moon*. The piece is really a vehicle for Gilmour to soar over the rooftops while the group maintains a solid, even slightly funky, beat. The lyrics, like all the others on *Meddle*, are in no way memorable; what counts are the sonic textures, the changing atmospheres: a blustery night on Grantchester Meadows? Do we even hear crows being blown around by the windy gusts? The creepy wailing of Rick's synthesiser, the layers of misty textures, all combine to build one of Pink Floyd's most memorable and solid pieces. Out of the swirling mist emerges that throbbing, bleeping, trademark something from miles away that is the Floyd rhythm section in full echo. It is a tremendous achievement, burned into the brain cells of a million revelers who listened to it the next morning while coming down from too much drink or drugs.

'Echoes' was not the only quintessential Floyd track on the album. 'One Of These Days' featured Syd's old Binson Echorec that even in the early Seventies could still get some delay effects that were not available elsewhere. David had used it on 'Echoes' and Roger decided to take some of the techniques that Gilmour had developed and try them on the bass. This was how he came up with the basic riff that powers 'One Of These Days'. It is the bass sound that makes the track. There was also another important piece of technology involved; an H&H amplifier set on vibrato. The opening section of the song features both David and Roger playing bass. The first bass is David, Roger comes in one bar later and the difference can easily be heard when listening through headphones.

This was the only Floyd track to feature Nick as vocalist, intoning the line, "One of these days, I'm going to cut you into little pieces," so altered that you would never know it was him. Nick was often amusing about his reticence as a singer: "Possibly the most interesting thing about 'One Of These Days' is that it actually stars myself as vocalist, for the first time on any of our records that actually got to the public. It's a rather startling performance involving the use of a high voice and slowed down tape."

The other tracks were less significant – indeed some regarded them as filler. 'St Tropez' could be a Randy Newman or Harry Nilsson outtake, whereas the joke of Rick's dog howling on the blues sing-a-long 'Seamus' soon stops being amusing after a few plays while 'A Pillow of Winds' could have been by any contemporary singer-songwriter. But 'Echoes' was undoubtedly a great leap forward.

Meddle appeared in November '71 and despite its undoubted improvement over *Atom Heart Mother*, it failed to climb higher than number three on the UK album charts.

[*]EMI Studios was notorious for its antiquated equipment and even when they did buy new machinery, it was already supplanted. The company finally upgraded to eight-tracks just as 16-track machines came in. The Pink Floyd's early albums were all done on four-track, with the consequent overdubbing and tape transfers reducing quality.

[*]The new recording doesn't kick in until the first chord change.

CHAPTER TWELVE
DARK SIDE OF THE MOON

CHAPTER TWELVE
DARK SIDE OF THE MOON

Dark Side Of The Moon marks the apogee of Pink Floyd's career. Even now, more than 30 years later, the album has hardly dated, with the possible exception of the sound of cash registers on 'Money' which few younger listeners would recognise. The shared experience of being on the road for seven years had created a closeness that the Floyd never had before, and would not have again. They were working well together and there was an unprecedented creative collaboration and sharing of ideas between them. This solidarity could be said to be responsible for much of the album's quality and subsequent success.

In addition the 'Eclipse' suite – as it was still known – had been performed live enough times for it to have grown and developed and for most of the wrinkles to be ironed out. They already recognised it as being their finest work and expected it to do well, but no one could have predicted its tremendous worldwide success, as David said, "The whole thing was a very powerful package, you know. We knew before we finished it that that it was definitely going to do a lot better than anything we'd done before. I mean we didn't think that it would do *that* well."

Dark Side Of The Moon did not appear fully formed. In September 1971 the band thought it was about time they undertook an English tour but felt that they couldn't book any dates unless they had some fresh material to perform. Ideally they liked the concerts to consist of new material in the first half, followed by a selection of earlier songs. The Floyd toured the States until the end of November and the first UK date was pencilled in for January 20, 1972. As usual the band was desperate for ideas. After some unproductive messing around in a scruffy warehouse owned by the Rolling Stones in Bermondsey, south London, the band met at their favourite rehearsal studio, a place on Broadhurst Gardens near West Hampstead tube station, and began to go through the scraps and bits and pieces they had left over from previous albums to see if anything could be salvaged.

Roger: "Everything we got together we immediately put on the Revox. At the end of four days we'd got half a dozen short pieces of music. It was exactly the same technique we used when we put together *Meddle*. Just putting ideas down... We sat in a little room and played our instruments, and we got quite a lot of stuff together – music – no lyrics, or ideas or anything. We had all these different pieces, like the riff of 'Money' came out of those sessions, and so on and so forth."

Rick: "At the start we only had vague ideas about madness being a theme. We rehearsed a lot just putting down ideas and then in the next rehearsals we used them. It flowed really well. There was a strong thing in it that made it easier to do." Wright was responsible for the music on five of the 10 tracks on the album – possibly the only time he felt fully integrated into the group and he was responding to the task well.

DARK SIDE OF THE MOON
PINK FLOYD DWARFED BY THEIR STAGE SHOW

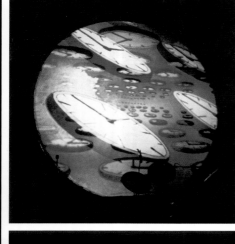

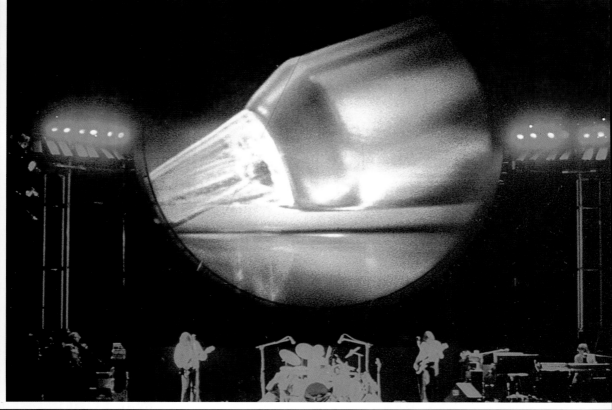

The band had Christmas off with their families and reconvened on New Year's Day 1972 in Nick Mason's kitchen in Highbury, north London. It was there Roger presented his idea of an album based on a theme of work, madness, aging and death.

Roger: "I'd been listening to songs and we thought we could do a whole thing about the pressures we personally feel that tend to drive one over the top, to drive one into crazy situations. So after that it was just really a question of sitting down and writing a few headings like – all this travelling about – money – the pressure of earning money. The time thing, time passing by very fast. The thing about organised power structures like the church or politics, violence, aggression. I sat down with that list of things having talked to mainly Nick about it, and just saying that we could work with that bit and go in that order."

Nick: "The album was going to be about... what we felt were the stress and strain of our lives and what was wrong with them or what we were motivated by and so on. And so we ended with a piece of paper upon which was written various subjects that would be covered, and worked from there. There wasn't any sitting down and saying let's produce something so crystal clear and delightful that everyone will adore it."

Roger: "I thought, and said, "Listen, if it was some kind of theme that ran through it – y'know – life, with a heartbeat and that... and then you could have other bits coming in, like the pressures that tend to be anti-life – how about that?" And then we all started writing out a list of what those pressures might be. And that was that."

David: "Sometime after we had started and got quite a few pieces of music sort of formulated vaguely, Roger came up with the specific idea of going through all the things that people go through and what drives them mad, and from that moment obviously our direction slightly changed. We started tailoring the pieces we already had to fit that concept and Roger would tailor words in to fit the music that we had, and from that moment on, it had a new impetus to it... it is set out very simply and clearly; the ideas that are behind it and what it's trying to say, I think... Roger tried definitely in his lyrics to make them very simple, straightforward, and easy to understand."

Roger: "And then I started writing lyrics with all these different bits of music that all came from different people in the band... I started writing a series of sets of lyrics about the different things we talked about. It's all terribly simple!"

Some people might think that this wasn't a simple theme at all; it was after all, the whole human condition that the band was attempting to explain. Roger, as the self-appointed lyricist, wrote all the words. There is much debate about the importance of lyrics in Pink Floyd's work but clearly in this case the words gave the album its theme. *Dark Side...* is a great record both musically and lyrically and the lyrics contributed greatly towards its success: it is very much an album to listen to alone when the soaring anthemic melodies and almost religious sonorities can have a deep emotional effect.

The early to mid Seventies was the age of the singer-songwriter and albums by Leonard Cohen, James Taylor, Neil Young and the like constituted a whole separate bedsit and dorm market. The words are kept simple, too simple for my taste, but designed to get the message over in as straightforward a way as possible and in this Waters succeeds admirably. It was an ambitious subject.

Roger: "There are a number of things that impinge upon an individual that colour his view of existence. There are pressures that are capable of pushing you in one direction or another and these are some of them and whether they push you towards insanity, death, empathy, greed, whatever, there's something about the Newtonian view of that physics that might be interesting and it's what this album is about."

Waters might sound pretentious but he believed deeply in what he was writing about, it had long been his subject matter but it found its most successful form here; later work became too dark. The lyrics were perfect for the work; they appealed to adolescent and undergraduate angst, in their clumsy way they articulated the confusion and wonder of young people emerging, blinking and a little scared, from adolescence into adulthood. They gave form to the nameless fears and anxieties about the future, and what might happen to them. It was a very positive message; having presented a grim picture of life, Roger's lyrics also gave hope.

As he explained when interviewed for the documentary *The Making Of Dark Side Of The Moon*: "I think within the context of the music and within the context of the piece as a whole, people are prepared to accept that simple exhortation to be prepared to stand your ground and attempt to live your life in an authentic way." For him, *Dark Side Of The Moon* was "an expression of political, philosophical and humanitarian

Right: Obscured By Clouds was released in June, 1972.

empathy that was desperate to get out."

Though adolescents were not the only audience for *Dark Side*, each year brought a new crop of listeners for whom it was the audio equivalent of *On The Road* or *The Catcher In The Rye*. Musically it was a complicated piece and took some time to shake down into a coherent whole. David: "An awful lot of time went into writing it in rehearsal rooms, and when we first got it together, took it out and did it in shows, it changed all the time. I can't remember when the specific changes happened and cemented it into being."

Roger accepted the idea that much of its appeal was to adolescents. He told *Rolling Stone*: "It's very difficult to write 'Breathe, breathe in the air, don't be afraid to care,' without people going, 'Fucking wanker!' And I think that's what Radiohead and these other bands are attaching to. There is a purity in those records. The records are bought by people when they hit puberty, when it becomes important to us to attach to ideas. That's why people are still buying *Catcher In The Rye*: to help us discover how we think."

The Dark Side Of The Moon took about six weeks to write, though some pieces on the album were not added until they recorded it some time later and other parts changed pretty radically. The Floyd toured Britain in the spring of 1972 to great acclaim. Already there was such a buzz about the band that they didn't need to advertise; in fact their total advertising budget for the UK tour, according to promoter Peter Bowyer, was £13 which included money for a notice to let fans know that because a power cut had cancelled a date in Manchester they would be returning on another date. They played more than a dozen cities, and every seat, all 13,000 in the provinces, was sold by word-of-mouth. The tour culminated in four nights at the Rainbow Theatre in London, a series of concerts regarded by many as the turning point in Pink Floyd's career.

They used the occasion to showcase 'Eclipse', and pulled out all the stops. It took four roadies six hours to assemble nine tons of equipment on stage and 12,000 people saw the four performances which each sold out. The critics loved it; Pink Floyd were no longer a psychedelic space band, they were presenting complex modern music, closer to the electronic music of Luciano Berio, Pierre Henry or Pierre Schaeffer than to the psychedelic noodlings of the Grateful Dead, and their lyrics were no longer abstract random appropriations and vague felicities to suit the mood, they were about the fears and problems of ordinary people.

The *Financial Times* wrote: "If anyone else attempted a visual and aural assault it would be a disaster; the Floyd have the furthest frontiers of pop music to themselves."

The band was still underground but their fame and success was growing exponentially. A very professional looking bootleg of their Rainbow concerts was released called *Pink Floyd Live* which many people bought thinking it was their latest official release; sales apparently topped 120,000 copies. This was to be an ongoing problem for the band that they were never able to satisfactorily solve. Three weeks after the Rainbow, they were in Tokyo to begin a short Japanese tour but before that, they recorded another soundtrack.

LA VALLÉE

La Vallée aka *Obscured By Clouds* was the second Floyd film commission from Barbet Schroeder. Schroeder: "The reason Pink Floyd music was used in *La Vallée* was because the actors were people that were listening to Pink Floyd music, so that's why we used Pink Floyd. Because it fit the actors. I asked them to write different songs with different moods. Some of it I told them what I wanted and some of it they did themselves. When the LP came out I chose what I could use for the movie."

The soundtrack was recorded in just two weeks, February 23-29 and March 23-27 1972 at the 'Honky Chateau' as Elton John called it, the Chateau d'Herouville outside Paris. This rather overlooked album in the Floyd canon is a favourite of the band's. Nick thought it was "sensational" and David said, "I love that album. Yes, it was really fast, rapid stuff without any great need to make a concept out of it. That was when we'd just got the very first synthesiser ever invented, and we were playing with it, the EMS Synthi. And all you could do was tune it up to play a note, and then press it for it to play the note, like you couldn't play notes with a keyboard, not at that juncture. Or if you could, we didn't know how to. That was the first time we ever used any form of a synthesiser, was on *Obscured By Clouds*."

Apart from the inevitable slow building drone that opens it - the Floyd often had trouble starting songs - who would ever guess that David's 'Childhood's End' was a

Pink Floyd song? It's a classic early Seventies British rock song with a surprisingly biting guitar solo and makes you wonder what direction Gilmour might have taken had he not joined Pink Floyd. Roger's 'Free Four', despite its cynical treatment of such weighty themes as aging and death, has a jauntiness not normally associated with the Floyd and is also pinned down by another blistering solo. The possible reason the album is so free and energetic was because the band members were getting on so well and just went into the studio, quickly playing their way through the numbers with high energy and enthusiasm; they were still at heart fans of rock 'n' roll and it sounds as if they were having fun. It is further evidence that the band were in peak condition during the gestation period of *Dark Side Of The Moon.*

Back on the road, the Japanese tour was followed almost immediately by a 15-city American trek. The Floyd performed 'Eclipse' at all of these shows, honing it, perfecting the dynamic flow, identifying weak spots. By the time they went into the studio, they had a very good idea of what they wanted and were well rehearsed.

RECORDING DARK SIDE

Sessions for *Dark Side Of The Moon* began on June 1, 1972 at Abbey Road where the Floyd had use of EMI's newly installed 16-track. Though spread over a nine month period, they actually made the album quite quickly, spending no more than 36 days in the studio, a little over a month in total, usually in four or five day blocks, using both studios 2 and 3. By now the Floyd were old hands at using the recording studio as an instrument and they took full advantage of the facilities on offer. They knew the people there and they had a very good team, led by balance engineer Alan Parsons.

Nick told Tommy Vance: "Abbey Road was, by '73, a much easier place to work. I know a number of people have talked about what Abbey Road used to be like, and when we first went in there, it was a lot less friendly, a lot less approving of the rock business. It was felt that they made proper music there, and these weird gits came in and messed about... you know, it wasn't quite right. We were sort of 'B' class.... But, once the Beatles had been in and put their stamp on it, it really changed."

Tommy Vance: "It was like going to the BBC?"

Nick: "It was more like going to the Lubyanka, painted in that green, I believe, the secret police at least favour."

There is movie footage of them at work on the album in the *Live At Pompeii* film directed by Adrian Maben. This was a sort of anti-live concert film. So many bands had been filmed with a sea of adulatory fans waving their arms and lighters, and there was plenty of footage of Pink Floyd's extraordinary lightshow. Maben came up with the idea of them performing in a stunning location, a 2000 year old Roman stadium, with no audience at all; just the ghosts of the long gone citizens whose town had been wiped out by volcanic gas and falling lava in 79 AD.

Nick: "Initially we were supposed to do it in playback, but the conditions were such that we went all the way and played live. And I believe that the music, in that arena filled with dust and sunshine, and later on with wind and darkness, was of great quality."

Though they had finished making the film a year and a half before, it had taken so long in post production that it was already out of date. Maben wanted footage of the Floyd working on their next album to make it more commercial. The film crew set up at EMI Studios and captured some of the actual recording of *Dark Side Of The Moon.* Apart from some rather stilted conversation in the canteen nothing was staged for the film.

The *Dark Side Of The Moon* album opens with 'Speak To Me,' a collage of voices suggested by Roger and assembled by Nick who, because of his interest in tape recorder techniques, became the de facto project manager for the album. Nick: "Usually I take care of everything referring to the magnetic tapes problem. I'm really not able to write songs. What I often do is give suggestions to the orchestration of the melodies the others come up with. That's the reason why I often co-write songs in Pink Floyd."

In keeping with the theme of the album, Roger wanted to get actual people talking about life. The studio lights were dimmed, a microphone was positioned above a chair and a music stand arranged in front of it. Roger wrote out a series of questions, one on each card, and asked people to read the question and answer it. Then they could remove the card and see the next one but they were not allowed to read through the cards in advance so they did not know what the thread of the questions was going to be. First Alan Parsons had to get a level for their voice, so he would ask them "Speak to me," thus giving the track its title.*

The questions began innocuously enough with "What is your favourite colour?" but quickly moved on to "Do you fear death?", "Are you mad?" and "When did you last hit someone?" followed by "Were you in the right?" and "Would you do it again if the same thing happened?" First the Floyd's roadies Chris Adamson, 'Puddy' Watts, 'Liverpool Bobby' and 'Roger the Hat' – whose stoned cackle appears in 'On The Run' – and their girlfriends were interviewed, followed by Jerry Driscoll, the Irish doorman at EMI Studios and other members of staff. Paul McCartney and Wings were recording in one of the studios at the time so Henry McCullough and his wife were quizzed as well as Paul and wife Linda who were so used to being interviewed that they were unable to react spontaneously. David: "They were much too good at being evasive for their answers to be usable."

One question was "What does the dark side of the moon mean to you?" 'Dark Side' was still the original title of Roger's song 'Brain Damage' but some of the responses such as that of Jerry the doorman which appeared on the record, when heard in the context of the other tracks, made them consider it as the most obvious title.* There was a problem in that Medicine Head had released an album of that name the year before but, fortunately for the Floyd, it went nowhere and as titles cannot be copyrighted, the band felt free to use it themselves.

The lyrics for 'Breathe' relate straight back to the work that Roger did with Ron Geesin on the soundtrack for *The Body* which opened with the words: "Breathe, breathe in the air." It was a good lyric for the time, instead of just saying "love everybody" as most bands did then, Waters said "Don't be afraid to love everybody," a very different message.

The next track, 'On The Run' was one of the Floyd's most ground-breaking efforts which predicted the sampling and appropriation of sounds that would not occur in pop music until decades hence. It shows their complete mastery of sound effects and creates an astonishing multi-layered sonic environment into which they mix even more effects: a heartbeat, the sound of footsteps – assistant engineer Peter James walking up and down Studio 2 breathless in heavy shoes – a tannoy announcing flight departures and so on including the terrifying throbbing of what sounds like a military helicopter swooping low – the Vietnam war was still raging as they made the album, something Roger, if not the others, must have been acutely aware of. The narrative, such as there is one, was someone running for a plane. David produced the jet engine roar on his Strat but it took the synthesiser to crash the plane.

The 'On The Run' electronic sequence came in at the very last minute when the band was nearly finished recording. They had already taped an 'On The Run' section which was more like the guitar jam they performed live when that part was known as 'The Travel Sequence' but they all felt that this instrumental chunk sat uneasily in the overall piece. When taking delivery of a briefcase model EMS-1 synthesiser that had a sequencer built into the lid, the band were all shown how to use it and immediately began to experiment. David: "I was playing with the sequencer device attachment, and came up with this sound, which is the basic sound of it. Roger sort of heard it, came over and started playing with it, too. Then he actually put in the notes that we made... He made that little sequence up, but I had got the actual original sound and I actually was the one doing the controlling on the take that we used. Then we chucked all sorts of things over the top of it afterwards." The synthesiser solved all their problems as well as creating one of the most remarkable tracks on the album.

One of Alan Parsons' jobs as a staff engineer at EMI Studios was to record different things for the legendary sounds effects library. He had recently taken a full set of field equipment to a clock shop to tape scores of different clocks ticking and chiming for a quadraphonic sound effects album. When the Floyd came to record 'Time' he mentioned this to the band. David: "He said, 'Listen, I just did all these things, I did all these clocks,' and so we wheeled out his tape and listened to it and said, 'Great! Stick it on!' They copied a clock on to each of the 16 tracks of the multi-track and back timed them to make their chimes coincide, then mixed it down to stereo. The effect was stunning. The other great feature of this track is of course the drumming. Nick used roto-toms but they also spent some time experimenting with some very small tuned drums called boo-bans. The roto-toms gave the best effect. The sound of the clocks in full quadraphonic sound went on to become a much loved feature of the Floyd's live show.

'The Great Gig In The Sky' is perhaps the album's most emblematic track with its

* 'Speak To Me' was originally part of 'Breathe' but was separated off in order to give Nick a publishing credit.
* The album was still known as *Eclipse*.

beautiful melody and extraordinary singing by Clare Torry. Written originally for the live version of 'Eclipse' it was then accompanied by parodies of Ecclesiastes to show how religion might cause insanity. This idea was dropped – they did, after all, want to sell records in America – and when it came time to record it was simply thought of as a musical evocation of fear of death, in particular Rick's fear of death by a plane crash. It began when Wright was sitting in the studio, tinkering with some chords on the piano, and David or Roger commented, "That sounds nice. Maybe we could use that on the album." Encouraged, Rick went home and worked on it. By the time they came to record it, he knew it off by heart and it was recorded in just one session.

The memorable key change that makes the track special was something that Rick took from 'So What' on Miles Davis' *Kind Of Blue*, one of his all-time favourite albums. But after they had overdubbed the other instruments Roger was not satisfied and it was Parsons who suggested bringing in Torry, whom he had worked with on a Music For Pleasure (EMI's budget label) album of pop hits. Alan had been impressed by her vocals and thought she would be good at improvising to Rick's melody. 22-year-old Clare arrived at the studio on the Sunday evening of January 21. She knew little about Pink Floyd and she told John Harris: "They told me what the album was about: birth and death and everything in between. I thought it was rather pretentious to be honest." When she asked what they wanted her to sing they didn't know, all David could tell her was that it should be "emotional".

She tried the normal backing vocal fills of the "Oh baby" variety, but David didn't want that; they would have used Doris Troy for that type of sound. Then Clare decided to use her voice purely as an instrument and that was when the magic happened. She didn't know it was great at the time, in fact she was rather embarrassed at being asked to scream and moan; sounds halfway between orgasm and terror. But David kept urging her to be *more* emotional so she really let go. It was a short but draining session and Torry left the studio soaked in sweat. She told Harris that as far as she was concerned, "It seemed a bit screechy-screechy. I really thought it would never see the light of day."

With the addition of some judicious echo, she had succeeded beyond the band's wildest expectations and her contribution is one of the most memorable aspects of the album.* Though as far as the band were concerned the subject of 'The Great Gig In The Sky' concerned death, the listeners thought the opposite, and within just a few weeks of the album's release it became the most popular backing track for live sex shows in Amsterdam and, although no accurate statistics exist, it was also put to the same use in bedrooms across the world as one of the great all-time lovemaking accompaniment songs.

Unusually for the band, 'Money' was in 7/4 time. It was Roger's song and he brought it in more or less completed in the form of a bluesy, guitar pickin' number. David: "We just made up middle sections, guitar solos and all that stuff. We also invented some new riffs – we created a 4/4 progression for the guitar solo and made the poor saxophone player play in 7/4. It was my idea to break down and become dry and empty for the second chorus of the solo." The first solo was artificially double-tracked and for the final one Gilmour had to switch from his Fender Stratocaster to a Lewis which had two whole octaves, enabling him to reach notes that the Strat couldn't reach. It is the switch from 7/8 to 4/4 for the hard rock 'n' roll guitar solo that made the song so popular, that and the greasy saxophone solo. Dick Parry, an old friend of David's from Cambridge, and the only saxophone player the band knew, was contacted and played a superb, honking solo in the best King Curtis manner.

Gilmour also contributed technically to the production of 'Money'. Alan Parsons was filled with praise for David's studio work, telling *Circus* magazine: "I think he's the most technically minded of the four. He actually knows what's going on technically inside the control room, and he would often come up with ideas of his own for production of a track. One instance was the cash register sounds for 'Money'. Originally we were timing the beats with a click-track but we weren't getting it right. David came up with the idea of actually measuring out pieces of tape with a ruler... David was very much a force behind the production of *Dark Side Of The Moon*."

The sound effects used on 'Money' also contribute greatly to its appeal. Roger: "I thought it would be good as an introduction to create a rhythmic device using the sound of money. I had a two-track studio at home with a Revox recorder. My first wife was a potter and she had a big industrial food mixer for mixing up clay. I threw handfuls of coins and wads of torn-up paper into it. We took a couple of things off sound effects records too. The backing track was everyone playing together, a

*30 years on, when she had retired from professional singing, Torry decided to claim royalties for her contribution to the track. She had not pursued this during her career because she knew the penalty for being seen as a "troublemaker". Her claim was settled in 2005 in an out-of-court agreement the details of which she is prohibited from disclosing but henceforth the song is now credited to 'Wright/Torry'.

157

Wurlitzer piano through a wah wah, bass, drums and that tremolo guitar. One of the ways you can tell that it was done live as a band is that the tempo changes so much from the beginning to the end. It speeds up fantastically."

It's hard to believe that the Floyd had 'Us And Them' on hold ever since *Zabriskie Point* and had not used it. Back then this lyrical ballad was known as 'The Violent Sequence', written by Rick to accompany news footage of Americans cops beating up anti-war demonstrators but inexplicably Antonioni never used it; it was, according to the director, "Too sad, it makes me think of church!" Then, when the band was working on *Dark Side*, there was a section that needed filling and Rick's ballad fitted perfectly. Rick: "'Us And Them' was a little piano piece I had worked out. I played it for them; they liked it. Roger went into another room and started working on the lyrics." The long echo on the vocals is one of the peculiarities of this track that makes it so special because it introduces masses of space into the voice.

'Any Colour You Like' is just an organ fantasia followed by an old-style Floyd guitar vamp; the only filler track on the album but one that was needed for balance; it's lightweight psychedelic noodling lightens the tone before reaching 'Brain Damage'. This song, first called 'The Dark Side Of The Moon' used to be the finale of the 'Eclipse' suite when the band played it in late-'71. Roger: "I had actually written a song previously when we were finishing the *Meddle* album and I wrote this song called 'Dark Side Of The Moon' about the lunatic on the grass, and it had been running round my mind." Roger was inspired by the signs forbidding people to walk on the great lawn behind Kings College Chapel in Cambridge. To him it questioned the whole idea of who was sane and who was not; who, in their right mind, would go to the trouble to plant a wonderful grass lawn and then forbid anyone to use it? It was also, of course, about Syd, one of Roger's first attempts to write about his reclusive friend.

After they had performed it a few times live, Roger felt that this was not a complete enough resolution to the 'Eclipse' suite. Roger: "It seemed to *need* something at the end." That something was 'Eclipse', which Waters was very casual about, walking in one day and saying, "Oh, by the way, I've written an ending." Roger: 'The last thing I wrote on *Dark Side Of The Moon* was 'Eclipse': 'All that you touch and all that you see, all that you taste, all that you feel' So I was getting kind of Buddhist about it. So what caused it? I suppose all the un-Buddhist 'stuff' of living in a van, seeing what the world was like, and being faced with one's ambitions and what they actually 'were'.'

Floyd fans have engaged in a lively debate about the true meaning of this track ever since but it is a straightforward explication of the Waters world view. Roger: "There was no riddle. It's saying that all the good things in life are there for us to grasp, but that the influence of the dark forces in our natures prevents us from seizing them." Roger could not have chosen a more powerful image to end the album: the cold dead moon passing silently in front of the blazing life-giving sun, blocking out its Earth-sustaining energy. Roger: "When Doris Troy did her wailing on 'Eclipse' we knew it was the climactic ending we wanted... We knew we had the album in the bag."

The amiable working conditions did not extend to the mixing of the album, which quickly polarised into two camps, with David on one side and Roger on the other. David: "[Producer] Chris Thomas came in for the mixes, and his role was essentially to stop the arguments between me and Roger about how it should be mixed. I wanted *Dark Side* to be big and swampy and wet, with reverbs and things like that. And Roger was very keen on it being a very dry album. I think he was influenced a lot by John Lennon's first solo album (*Plastic Ono Band*), which was very dry. We argued so much that it was suggested we get a third opinion. We were going to leave Chris to mix it on his own, with Alan Parsons engineering. And of course on the first day I found out that Roger sneaked in there. So the second day I sneaked in there. And from then on, we both sat right at Chris' shoulder, interfering. But luckily, Chris was more sympathetic to my point of view than he was to Roger's."

By now the Floyd recognised that they had created something exceptional. Roger: "It sounded special. When it was finished, I took the tape home and played it to my first wife, and I remember her bursting into tears when she'd finished listening to it. And I thought, 'Yeah, that's kind of what I expected,' because I think it's very moving emotionally and musically. Maybe its humanity has caused *Dark Side* to last as long as it has."

It was not just the mix that was a cause for argument. Waters and Gilmour had a fundamental disagreement over the importance of lyrics. David told Tommy Vance: "My problem with *Dark Side* was that I thought Roger's emergence on that album as a great lyric writer was such that he came to overshadow the music in places, and there

Above: Dark Side Of The Moon was released in March, 1973.